THE EDEXCEL G
ANTHOLOGY: TIME & PLACE – THE
STUDENT GUIDE

DAVID WHEELER

Red Axe Books

ISBN: 978-1911477006

Find us at:

www.dogstailbooks.co.uk

CONTENTS

Introduction

What is your favourite place in the whole world? What is the place you dislike the most in the whole world? Is there a place or places that hold special memories for you or which you associate with some special event in your life? If so, then you will start to be in tune with many of the poems in this book. Almost all the poems in this section deal with a specific place that is important to the poet; many of them are set in the countryside, but there some with urban settings; some of these places prompt happy memories, but others evoke a sense of sadness or other less positive emotions.

I hope you find this revision guide useful. It consists of an individual analysis of each poem in the Edexcel GCSE Poetry Anthology – Place. The analysis of each poem follows the same pattern: there is a section on the poet and the context in which the poem was written and some facts about each author; unfamiliar words are explained; and then each poem has a commentary which focuses on both what the poem is about and the style, form and structure that the poet uses. A final section on each poem summarizes the poem's overall impact and effect. There are no colours, few illustrations, but you will get a clear sense of what each poem is about and each poem's overall effect.

Who or what is this book for?

Perhaps you missed that crucial lesson on one particular poem that you find hard to understand? Good lessons are better than this book, because through different activities and through careful questioning and probing your teacher will help you to arrive at an understanding, an appreciation of the poem that you work out for yourself – and that process is invaluable – it's a process of thinking and exploring as a group, in a pair perhaps and as an individual, and, no matter how good the notes that your class-mates made, those notes are no substitute for having been there and gone through the process of the lesson. So, maybe, through absence, you feel a little out of touch with some of the poems: this book will help you.

Alternatively, you may want to read about ideas which you have not encountered in class. Alternatively, you may have the sort of teacher who allows you to respond in your own way to the poems; that is a completely valid and worthwhile approach, of course, but it does not suit every student: some students like to have clear guidelines about the meaning of what they read and to have various interpretations suggested to them so that they are at least aware of the overall gist of the poem. It still leaves you free to make up your own mind and have your own ideas, but it does provide a starting point – this book will give you that starting point.

You may be trying to revise the poems in the final days and weeks before the exam and want a quick refresher on poems that you first studied in class a long time ago; maybe it was a Friday afternoon and you weren't paying complete attention; maybe you were late for the lesson and never quite 'got' what the poem is about; maybe you were distracted by something more interesting happening outside and spent the lesson gazing out of the window. This book will help you get to grips with those poems.

It is very unlikely, but you may be reading these poems on your own for the very first time – this book will help you too, because I have assumed that you know nothing about the poem or about poetry, and the commentary on each poem is written so that you can start from scratch. Of course, some of you might find this a tiny bit condescending – and I apologize for that. I should also apologize if there are ideas in this book which are different from ones you have encountered before in class. There are as many different ways to read a poem as there are readers, and each reader might have a slightly different view of a particular poem – as we shall see.

So... if you want a book that tells you what each poem means; comments on features of style and structure; suggests the tone or the overall impact of each poem; gives you the necessary background knowledge to understand each poem – then this is it. At the end you will find a glossary of poetic terms, but after this introduction, there is a commentary on each poem – each commentary is self-contained and can be read on its own. Throughout the book I have used the words that I would use if I were teaching a lesson on these poems – if I use words you don't know or haven't heard, then look them up. Part of education, part of writing well about Literature is the way you yourself write, so to expand your vocabulary is a good thing. Terms which have specific literary meanings are all in the glossary at the back of the book.

Help Yourself!

I hope you find this book helpful in some ways, perhaps many ways. It deliberately does not include very detailed information about the authors for two reasons. Firstly, it would be a waste of space. Secondly, the internet is a rich source of information about writers and their work – an internet search on any of your studied poets or poems will throw up all sorts of interesting resources, including student chat boards, online revision chat-rooms as well as more obvious sources of information like Wikipedia or web sites associated with a particular author. Where there is detailed biographical information here, it is because it is vital to an understanding of the poem.

But do be warned – all the information you can possibly find about a particular poet may help to clarify something you already sensed about the poem, but it is no substitute for engagement with the poem itself. And in the examination the examiner does <u>not</u> want to read a potted biography of the poet whose poem you have chosen to write about. Besides - generalizing from what we know about a writer or his/her era is a dangerous thing: for example, it is important to be aware of William Blake's political beliefs and to be aware that he wrote 'London' (in the Anthology) and 'The Sick Rose' (discussed in this introduction) during the years of the French Revolution – some might say that without such an awareness the poem cannot be fully appreciated and understood – BUT that will not help you explain the impact of individual words and lines and images at all, nor will it help you write well in the examination.

Very often I have started my commentary on a poem with necessary information to help you understand it, but you don't need to reproduce all that information in the exam - it is there to help you fully understand significant details about the poem; to try to reproduce the process of discovery that a good lesson will guide you through. But it probably has little place in the examination.

You may be the sort of student who is doing English Language or English Literature because it is compulsory at your school. But it may also be that as you progress through the course you come to feel that English is a subject that you like and are good at; you may even be intrigued or fascinated by some of the poems in the anthology. If that happens, then do not rely on this book. Look on the internet for resources that will further your interest. For example, if one poet makes a special impact on you – read some of their other work; you will find a lot of it available on-line. Many of the poets in the Literary Heritage sections are now out of copyright – their work is freely available on-line. Many of the contemporary poets have their own websites which can be a fascinating source of extra information and contain links to other poems or biographical information. So there are many ways in which you can help yourself: it's a good habit to get into, especially if you start thinking about the possibility of doing English at A level.

But please remember this is no substitute for a close engagement with the poems themselves. And just as importantly – this book is no substitute for a good lesson which allows you to think about the poem's language and ideas, and then slowly come to an understanding of it. After understanding it (and that is an emotional as much as a logical understanding of it), you may come to appreciate it. What does that mean? Well, as you go through the course and read more and more poems then you may find that you prefer some to others. The next step is to identify why you prefer some poems to others: in this there are no right answers, but there are answers which are clearer and better expressed than others. And preference must be based on reasons to do with the way the poem is written or its overall emotional impact: it's your job to put what you think and feel into words – I cannot help you do that. I can merely point out some of the important features and meanings of the poems. As you grow in confidence and perhaps read other writing on these poems or listening to your teacher or your classmates, then you will start to formulate your own opinions – stealing an idea from one person, a thought from somewhere else and combining all these different things into your own view of the poem. And that is appreciation. As soon as you say you prefer one poem to another you are engaging in a critical reaction to what you have read – in exactly the same way that people prefer one film to another or one song or performer to another.

Romanticism

In this cluster of poems the first three are designated Romantic poems and it is important that you have an understanding of what Romanticism was. It has very little to do with the word 'romantic' as we apply it today to an event like Valentine's Day.

Romanticism is the name given to the artistic, political and cultural movement that emerged in England and Germany in the 1790s and in the rest of Europe in the 1820s and beyond. It was a movement that saw great changes in literature, painting, sculpture, architecture and music, and found its catalyst in the new philosophical ideas of Jean Jacques Rousseau and Thomas Paine, and in response to the American, French and industrial revolutions. Its chief emphasis was on freedom of individual self-expression, sincerity, spontaneity and originality, but it also looked to the distant past of the Middle Ages for some of its inspiration. In Romantic thought the nature of the poet changed: no longer was a poet someone who could manipulate words well and with skill; the poet was a special individual with a unique vision to communicate and with special insights to communicate through his poetry.

The key characteristics of Romantic poetry in English are:

- a reverence for and veneration of the natural world.
- a belief that the poet was a special person who had important truths to communicate and whose experiences were more intense than those of ordinary people.
- an emphasis on individualism and intense emotion.
- an increased interest in ordinary people – the rural poor and the urban working classes.
- a political radicalism, best summed up by the watchwords of the French Revolution – liberty, fraternity, equality.
- an overwhelming emphasis on the sensibility and imagination of the poet.
- an interest in medieval and ancient history.
- a veneration of Shakespeare.
- a desire to be original and to reject the orthodoxies of the immediate past.

Of course, not all the poets that we label 'Romantic' displayed all these characteristics all through their careers.

Contemporary Poetry & the Literary Heritage

You will probably have noticed that the poems within each section or cluster of your anthology are designated as Literary Heritage poems. Why? Contemporary poetry consists of poems written in the very recent past by living poets and they are here because as you study English or English Literature, it is felt to be important that you realize that poetry is not dead and poetry is not only written by dead white Englishmen: it is alive and it is being written now all over the English-speaking world by men and by women from a wide variety of backgrounds. So the contemporary poems are there to remind you that poetry is alive and well and thriving. Indeed, as I have already mentioned, many of the contemporary poets have their own websites or perform poetry readings which you may be lucky enough to attend during your course. You can also see some performances of these poems on the internet.

The poems in the first half of the anthology are generally by dead white Englishmen, although there are some poems by women. That sounds dismissive (dead white Englishmen), but it's not meant to be. They are in the anthology to remind you that writers have been writing poetry in English for hundreds of years and that what happens over those centuries is that an agreement emerges about which poems are some of the greatest or most significant ever written in the English Language. How does such agreement emerge? Well, mainly through people continuing to read the poems, responding to them and enjoying them; another concrete way is for the poems to appear in anthologies – which ensures them an even wider audience. The point you need to grasp is that writing in English poetry has been going on for hundreds of years and what has been written in the past influences what is written now. Many contemporary poets will have read the poems that you will read in the Literary Heritage sections. So when you read, for example, 'Exposure' by Wilfred Owen for the first time, you will be joining the millions of English-speaking people all over the world who have read and responded to that poem. Organizations like the BBC have also run public votes where members of the public can vote for their favourite poem – another way that we know which poems are popular. Such poems then become part of the canon. That is not to say, however, that there is only agreement about the value of poems from the distant past: some like those by Grace Nichols and U A Fanthorpe are from the closing decades of the 20th century; they are included because already there is widespread agreement that these poets are important and influential and that their poems are rewarding to read and study and enjoy.

So part of our heritage, part of the culture of speaking English, whether you speak English in Delhi or London or Manchester or Lahore or Trinidad or Liverpool or Auckland or Toronto or Cape Town or Chicago, is centuries of English poetry and a continuing poetic culture which is rich and vibrant, and includes voices from all over the English-speaking world.

The Secret of Poetry

The secret of poetry, of course, is that there is no secret. Nonetheless, I have come across lots of students who find poetry challenging or off-putting or who don't like it for some reason. I find this attitude bizarre for all sorts of reasons. But some students are very wary of poetry or turned off by it. If you are – rest assured: you shouldn't be!

Poetry is all around us: in proverbial sayings, in popular music, in the nursery rhymes we listen to or sing as children, in playground skipping chants, even in the chanting heard at football matches. All these things use the basic elements of poetry: rhythm and rhyming and very often the techniques of poetry – alliteration, repetition, word play. Advertisements and newspaper headlines also use these techniques to make what they say memorable. Ordinary everyday speech is full of poetry: if you say that something is 'as cheap as chips' you are using alliteration and a simile; if you think someone is 'two sandwiches short of a picnic', if someone is 'a pain in the arse', then you are using metaphors – the only difference is that when poets use similes and metaphors they try to use ones that are fresh and original – and memorable, in the same away that a nursery rhyme or your favourite song lyrics are memorable. Even brand names or shop names use some of the techniques of poetry: if you have a Kwik Fit exhaust supplier in your town you should note the word-play (the mis-spelling of Kwik) and the assonance – the repetition of the 'i' sound. There must be several hundred ladies' hairdressers in the UK called 'Curl Up and Dye' – which is comic word-play. You may go to 'Fat Face' because you like what they sell, but I hope that when you go next time, you'll spare a thought for the alliteration and assonance in the shop's name.

Poets also play with words. So when students tell me they don't like poetry, I don't believe them – I feel they have simply not approached it in the right way. Or perhaps not seen the link between the poetry of everyday life and the poetry they have to study and analyze for GCSE.

Poetry has been around a very long time: the earliest surviving literature in Europe consists of poetry. As far as we can tell poetry existed even before writing, and so poems were passed down by word of mouth for centuries before anyone bothered to write them down. If something is going to be passed down and remembered in this way, then it has to be memorable. And, as we shall see, poets use various techniques and tricks and patterns to make what they write easy to remember or striking in some way - just as you may remember the words to your favourite song or to a nursery rhyme that was recited to you as a small child. Let us take one example. The opening sentence of Charles Dickens' novel *A Tale of Two Cities* is

It was the best of times; it was the worst of times.

It is not poetry, but it is very memorable, because Dickens uses simple repetition, parallelism and paradox to create a very memorable sentence. Parallelism because the two halves of the sentence are the same — except for one word; and paradox because the two words — best and worst — seem to contradict each other. Now look at this recent slogan from an advert for Jaguar cars:

Don't dream it. Drive it.

This uses the same techniques as Dickens: parallelism and paradox (or juxtaposition) and it also uses alliteration. It is all about manipulating words to give them greater impact — to make them memorable.

As I am sure I will repeat elsewhere, it is always vital to read a poem aloud: your teacher might do it very well, you might be lucky enough to hear one of the living poets in the anthology read their poems aloud or you can access many recordings via the internet. I think reading a poem aloud is a good way to revise it: it has been claimed that when we read something aloud we are reading twenty times slower than when we read with our eyes — and that slowness is vital, because it allows the sound of the poem, the turn of each phrase and the rhythm of each poem to stand out. As we shall see, the way a poem sounds is absolutely crucial to its impact — for one thing, it helps you pick out techniques such as alliteration and assonance.

One of the things we will discover is that poetry is partly about pattern – patterns of sounds, of words, of rhythm; patterns of lay-out too, so that a poem and the way it is set out on the page - often separated into separate stanzas (don't call them verses) – is vital. If you quickly glance at a page from the anthology, you would probably assume that what is on the page is a poem – because we have certain expectations of the way that poems look. So what? You have probably been aware for a long time that poets often organize what they write into stanzas. For me this is an absolutely crucial part of poetry because as human beings we are in love with patterns, we are addicted to patterns – and that is one of the many reasons we love poetry or find it so appealing. Patterns dominate our lives. We may have patterns on our clothes, our furnishings, our curtains, our carpets. But patterns rule our lives more completely than that: seen from above even a housing estate has patterns – the street lights at regular intervals, the garages and gardens in the same relationship to the houses; a spider's web on a frosty morning; the unique patterns of snowflakes; a honeycomb; your school uniform perhaps; the rhythm of your day, of the timetable you follow at school, of your week, of the seasons and of the year. And where patterns do not exist we like to invent them: the periodic table of elements (which you may be familiar with from Chemistry) does not exist as a table out there in nature – it's the human need to organize and give things a pattern which is responsible for the way it looks. Or look at a map of the world, criss-crossed by lines of longitude and latitude – and invented by the human mind as an aid for navigation.

What on earth has this to do with poetry? Well, poetry, especially from the past, likes to follow patterns and this structure that poets choose is something we instinctively like; it is also important when poets set up a pattern, only to break it to make whatever they are saying even more memorable because it breaks the pattern. We will see this happen in some of the poems in the anthology.

Let us look at it another way. Take the sonnet: if you choose to write a sonnet, you are committing yourself to trying to say what you want to say in 140 syllables, arranged in equal lines of 10 syllables each and fitted to a complex rhyming scheme. It is very hard to do, so why bother? Partly because it is a challenge – to force you to condense what you want to say into 140 syllables concentrates the mind and, more importantly, makes for language that can be very condensed and full of meaning. And, of course, the sonnet has been around for centuries so to choose to write one now means you are following (and hoping to bring something new and surprising) to a long-established form.

So what is poetry? *The Oxford Concise Dictionary of Literary Terms* defines it as:

Language sung, chanted, spoken, or written according to some pattern of recurrence that emphasizes the relationships between words on the basis of sound as well as sense: this pattern is almost always a rhythm or metre, which may be supplemented by rhyme or alliteration or both. All cultures have their poetry, using it for various purposes from sacred ritual to obscene insult, but it is generally employed in those utterances and writings that call for heightened intensity of emotion, dignity of expression, or subtlety of meditation. Poetry is valued for combining pleasures of sound with freshness of ideas....

Remember some of these phrases as you read this book or as you read the poems in the Anthology – which poems have intensity of emotion? Are there some which have a freshness of ideas? Or do some make you think about things more deeply (subtlety of meditation)? Perhaps there are poems which make you do all three? What can I possibly add to the Oxford Book of Literary Terms? Think of your favourite song – whatever type of music you listen to. The song's lyrics will share many of the characteristics of poetry, but the words will be enhanced by the music and the delivery of the vocalist. Is it a song that makes you happy or sad? Angry or mellow? Whatever it makes you feel, a song takes you on an emotional journey – and that is what poems do too, except they lack musical accompaniment. So think of a poem as being like a song –

designed to make you feel a particular emotion and think particular thoughts; like some songs, the emotions, the thoughts, may be quite complex and hard to explain but the similarity is there. And that is another reason why it is important to hear the poems read aloud – they are designed to be listened to, not simply read. Short poems like the ones in the Anthology are often called lyric poems – and that is because hundreds of years ago they would have been accompanied by music. Before 1066 Anglo-Saxon bards telling even long narrative poems used to accompany themselves on a lyre – a primitive type of guitar and up to Elizabethan times lyric poems were set to music and performed.

Making Connections

As you can see from what is written above, a lot of the work in English on the Anthology is about making connections – the exam question will explicitly ask you to do this. As you study the Anthology or read this book you should try to make connections for yourself. Free your mind and make unusual connections. You might feel that some poems take you on a similar emotional journey; some poems might use metaphor or personification in similar ways; some poems were written at the same time as others and are connected by their context.

If you can connect poems because of their written style or something like structure or technique, then that will impress the examiner more than if you simply connect them by subject matter. The poems are already connected by simply being in the Anthology, so to start an answer, for example, by stating that two poems are about 'Place' is a waste of words. You should try to do some thinking for yourself as you read this book and reflect on the poems in the anthology– because it is a good habit to get into and helps prepare you mentally for the exam.

Do you have a favourite word? If you do, you might like to think about why you like it so much. It may well have something to do with the meaning, but it might also have something to do with the sound. Of course, some words are clearly onomatopoeic like *smash*, *bang* and *crack*. But other words have sound qualities too which alter the way we react to them – and they are not obviously onomatopoeic. For example, the word *blister* sounds quite harsh because the letter *b* and the combination of *st* sound a little unpleasant; and, of course, we know what a *blister* is and it is not a pleasant thing. On the other hand, words like *fearful* or *gentle* or *lightly* have a lighter, more delicate sound because of the letters from which they are made. Words like *glitter* and *glisten* cannot be onomatopoeic: onomatopoeia is all about imitating the sound that something makes and *glitter* and *glisten* refer to visual phenomena, but the *gl* at the start and the *st* and *tt* in the middle of the words make them sound entirely appropriate, just right, don't they?

Think of it another way: just reflect on the number of swear words or derogatory terms in English which start with *b* or *p*: *bloody, bugger, bastard, plonker, pratt, prick, prawn* – the list goes on and on. The hard *c* sound in a word like *cackle* is also unpleasant to the ear. So what? Well, as you read poems try to be aware of this, because poets often choose light, gentle sounds to create a gentle atmosphere: listen to the sounds. Of course, the meaning of the word is the dominant element that we respond to, but listen to it as well.

You don't need to know anything about the history of the English language to get a good grade at GCSE. However, where our language comes from makes English unique. English was not spoken in the British Isles until about 450 CE when tribes from what is now Holland invaded as the Roman Empire gradually collapsed. The language these tribes spoke is now known as Old English – if you were to see some it would look very foreign to your eyes, but it is where our basic vocabulary comes from. A survey once picked out the hundred words that are most used in written English: ninety-nine of them had their roots in Old English; the other one was derived from French. The French the Normans spoke had developed from Latin and so when we look at English vocabulary – all the words that are in the dictionary – we can make a simple distinction between words that come from Old English and words that come from Latin – either directly from Latin or from Latin through French. [I am ignoring for the moment all the hundreds of thousands of words English has adopted from all the other languages in the world.]

So what? I hear you think. Well, just as the sounds of words have different qualities, so do the words derived from Old English and from Latin. Words that are Old English in origin are short, blunt and down-to-earth; words derived from Latin or from Latin through French are generally longer and sound more formal. Take a simple example: house, residence, domicile. *House* comes from Old English; *residence* from Latin through French and *domicile* direct from Latin. Of course, if you invited your friends round to your residence, they would probably think you were sounding rather fancy – but that is the whole point. We associate words of Latinate origin with formality and elegance and sometimes poets might use words conscious of the power and associations that they have. Where a poet has used largely Latinate vocabulary it creates a special effect and there are poems in the Anthology where I have pointed this feature out. Equally, the down to earth simplicity of words of English origin can be robust and strong.

Alliteration is a technique that is easy to recognize and is used by many poets and writers to foreground their work. It can exist, of course, in any language. However, it seems to have appealed to writers in English for many centuries. Before 1066 when the Normans invaded and introduced French customs and culture, poetry was widely written in a language we now call Old English, or Anglo Saxon. Old English poetry did not rhyme. How was it patterned then? Each line had roughly the same number of syllables, but what was more important was that each line had three or four words that alliterated. Alliterative poetry continued to be written in English until the 14th century and if you look at these phrases drawn from everyday English speech I think you can see that it has a power even today: busy as a bee, cool as a cucumber, good as gold, right as rain, cheap as chips, dead as a doornail, kith and kin, hearth and home, spick and span, hale and hearty. Alliteration can also be found in invented names. Shops: Coffee Corner, Sushi Station, Caribou Coffee, Circuit City. Fictional characters: Peter Pan, Severus Snape, Donald Duck, Mickey Mouse, Nicholas Nickleby, Humbert Humbert, King

Kong, Peppa Pig. The titles of films and novels: *Pride and Prejudice, Sense and Sensibility, Debbie Does Dallas, House on Haunted Hill, Gilmour Girls, V for Vendetta, A Christmas Carol, As Good as it Gets, The Witches of Whitby, The Wolf of Wall Street.* Alliteration is an easy way to make words and phrases memorable.`

So what? Well, as you read the poems and see alliteration being used, I think it is helpful to bear in mind that alliteration is not some specialized poetic technique, but is part of the fabric of everyday English too and it is used in everyday English for the same reasons that it is used by poets – to make the words more memorable.

An Approach to Poetry

This next bit may only be relevant if you are studying the poems for the first time and it is an approach that I use in the classroom. It works well and helps students get their bearing when they first encounter a poem. These are the Five Ws. They are not my idea, but I use them in the classroom all the time. They are simply five questions which are a starting point, a way of getting into the poem and a method of approaching an understanding of it. With some poems some of the answers to the questions are more important than others; with some poems these questions and our answers to them will not get us very far at all – but it is where we will start. I will follow this model with each commentary. They are also a good way to approach the unseen poem. With one exception, I have chosen poems in which the notion of place is important. The five questions to ask of each poem you read are:

- Who?

- When?

- Where?

- What?

- Why?

WHO? Who is in the poem? Whose voice the poem uses? This is the first and most basic question. In many poems the poet speaks as themselves, but sometimes they are ventriloquists – they pretend to be someone else. So first of all we must identify the voice of the poem. We must ask ourselves to whom the poem is addressed. It isn't always right to say – the reader; some poems are addressed to a particular individual. And, of course, there may well be other people mentioned in the poem itself. Some poetry is quite cryptic, so who 'you' and 'they' are in a poem make a crucial difference to the way we interpret it. Why are poems 'cryptic'? Well, one reason is that they use language in a very compressed way – compressed perhaps because of the length of each line or the decision to use rhyme.

WHEN? When was the poem written and when is it set? This is where context is important. We know our context: we are reading the poem now, but when the poem was written and when the poem is set (not always the same, by any means) is crucial to the way we interpret it. The gender or background of the poet might be important, the society they were living in, the circumstances which led them to write the poem – all these things can be crucial to how we interpret the poem.

WHERE? Where is the poem set? Where do the events described in the poem take place? With some poems this question is irrelevant; with others it is absolutely vital – it all depends on the poem. In the Anthology you will find some poems which depend on some understanding of where they are set for them to work; you will find other poems where the location is not specified or is irrelevant or generalized – again it depends on the poem.

WHAT? This means what happens in a poem. Some poems describe a place; some describe a particular moment in time; some tell a story; some have a story buried beneath their surface; some make statements – some may do several or all of these things at once. They are all potentially different, but what happens is something very basic and should be grasped before you can move on to really appreciate a poem. Very often I have kept this section really short, because it is only when you start to look closely at language that you fully understand what is going on.

WHY? This is the hardest question of all and the one with a variety of possible answers, depending on your exact view of the poem in question. I like to think of it as asking ourselves 'Why did the poet write this poem?' Or 'What is the overall message or emotional impact of this poem?' To answer it with every poem, we need to look at all the other questions, the way the poet uses language and its effect on us, and try to put into words the tone of the voice of the poem and the poem's overall impact. Students in the classroom often seem puzzled by my asking them to discuss the poem's tone. But it boils down to this - if you were reading the poem out loud, what tone of voice would you use? What is the mood or atmosphere of the poem? Does the poet, or whoever the poet is pretending to be, have a particular attitude to what he or she is writing about? Answering these questions helps us discuss the tone of the poem. But you may not agree with everybody else about this and this is good: through disagreement and discussion, our understanding of what we read is sharpened. In the commentaries on each poem in this Anthology this question 'Why?' is answered at the very end of each commentary, because it is only after looking closely at the poet's use of language, form and structure that we can begin to answer it. If you feel you know the poem well enough, you might just use the section 'Why?' for each poem as a quick reminder of what its main message is. For all the poems the 'Why?' section consists of a series of bullet points which attempt to give you the words to express what the poem's main point is.

A Word of Warning

This book and the commentaries on individual poems that follow are full of words to do with literature – the technical devices such as metaphor, simile, oxymoron. These are the vocabulary to do with the craft of writing and it is important that you understand them and can use them with confidence. It is the same as using the word *osmosis* in Biology or *isosceles* in Maths. However, in the examination, it is absolutely pointless to pick out a technique unless you can say something vaguely intelligent about its effect – the effect is vital! The examiner will know when a poet is using alliteration and does not need you to point it out; the sort of writing about poetry that consists of picking out technical devices and saying nothing about their effect or linking them in some meaningful way to the subject matter is worthless. I will suggest, in each commentary, what the effect might be, but we can generalize and say that all techniques with words are about making the poem memorable in some away – and this 'making something memorable' is also about foregrounding language. Language that is foregrounded means that it is different from normal everyday language and that it draws attention to itself by being different – it would be like if we all went round every day and tried to use a metaphor and alliteration in everything that we said or if we tried speaking in rhyme all day – people would notice!

Warming Up

Before we look at any of the poems from the anthology, I want to briefly examine two poems to give you a taste of the approach that will be followed throughout the rest of the book. So we will start by looking at two completely different poems. I am not going to subject either to a full analysis, but I will demonstrate with both poems some crucial ways of reading poetry and give you some general guidance which will stand you in good stead when we deal with the poems in the anthology itself. This is not meant to confuse you, but to help. I cannot stress enough that these poems are not ones that you will be assessed on. They are my choice – and I would use the same method in the classroom – introducing a class very slowly to poetry and 'warming up' for the anthology by practising the sorts of reading skills which will help with any poem. Besides, you may find the method valuable in your preparation for answering on the unseen poem in the exam.

Here is the first poem we will consider. It is by William Wordsworth and is an extract from a poem called 'The Prelude' and it describes what happens when the poet, as a young boy, steals a boat for a furtive row on a lake in the English Lake District:

One summer evening (led by her) I found
A little Boat tied to a Willow-tree
Within a rocky cave, its usual home.
Straight I unloosed her chain, and stepping in
Pushed from the shore. It was an act of stealth
And troubled pleasure, nor without the voice
Of mountain-echoes did my boat move on,
Leaving behind her still, on either side,
Small circles glittering idly in the moon,
Until they melted all into one track
Of sparkling light. But now, like one who rows,
(Proud of his skill) to reach a chosen point
With an unswerving line, I fixed my view
Upon the summit of a craggy ridge,
The horizon's utmost boundary; far above
Was nothing but the stars and the grey sky.
She was an elfin Pinnace; lustily
I dipped my oars into the silent lake,
And, as I rose upon the stroke, my boat
Went heaving through the Water like a swan;
When, from behind that craggy Steep till then
The horizon's bound, a huge peak, black and huge,
As if with voluntary power instinct,
Upreared its head.—I struck and struck again,
And growing still in stature the grim Shape
Towered up between me and the stars, and still,
For so it seemed, with purpose of its own
And measured motion like a living Thing,
Strode after me. With trembling oars I turned,
And through the silent water stole my way

Back to the Covert of the Willow-tree;
There in her mooring-place I left my Bark,—
And through the meadows homeward went, in grave
And serious mood; but after I had seen
That spectacle, for many days, my brain
Worked with a dim and undetermined sense
Of unknown modes of being; o'er my thoughts
There hung a darkness, call it solitude
Or blank desertion. No familiar Shapes
Remained, no pleasant images of trees,
Of sea or Sky, no colours of green fields;
But huge and mighty Forms, that do not live
Like living men, moved slowly through the mind
By day, and were a trouble to my dreams.

'The Prelude' (stealing the boat) – William Wordsworth

Context

William Wordsworth was born in 1770 in Cockermouth on the edge of the English Lake District. He had a life-long fascination with nature and it is from the natural world that he took much of his inspiration. He died in 1850, having been made Poet Laureate in 1843. Wordsworth began to write *The Prelude* in 1798 and kept working on it and revising it until his death. It was not published until 1850, three months after his death. He published many poems during his own lifetime, but many readers feel that *The Prelude* is his finest work.

This extract is from *The Prelude*, a long autobiographical poem first finished in 1805. It is subtitled *The Growth of the Poet's Mind* – and Wordsworth tells the story of his life, but with the intention of showing his psychological development and also how he came to be a poet. Central to his development, he claims, was the influence of nature: Wordsworth grew up in the English Lake District – a national park and an area of outstanding natural beauty even today. It is not just that Wordsworth liked the beauty of nature – we perhaps all do that because we associate it with peace, away from the hustle and bustle of urban or suburban life; he also believed that nature had a moral influence on him and had made him a better human being. He is at pains throughout *The Prelude* to try and prove this connection – that his experiences in the natural world made him a better person and a poet. You may elsewhere read references to Wordsworth's pantheism. Pantheists worship nature and feel that if there is a God then that God exists in every living thing, every part of the natural world: God is a spirit of the universe which exists in a rock or a daffodil as much as it does in a human being.

her – Nature.

elfin pinnace – a pinnace is a small boat; elfin means small and charming.

covert – secret.

bark – boat.

Who? The poet narrates in the past tense an incident from his childhood.

When? 1805. Wordsworth was a child in the late 18th century, but is recollecting this experience as an adult.

Where? On a lake in the English Lake District, generally thought to be Ullswater.

What? Wordsworth steals a boat and goes for a row on the lake. He explores the ramifications of this incident on his conscience.

Commentary

This extract is written in blank verse. It narrates an incident. This extract comes from Book II of *The Prelude* which is entitled *Childhood and School-Time*. The opening sentence clearly shows the influence of Nature on the young Wordsworth:

One summer evening (led by her) I found

A little boat tied to a willow tree.

We know that *her* refers to nature from the preceding lines. The poet proceeds to unchain the boat and take it for an illicit row on the lake. In effect, Wordsworth is stealing the boat: he describes it as *an act of stealth* (he doesn't want to get caught) and uses an oxymoron - *troubled pleasure* – to show us that he has mixed feelings about what he is doing: he knows it is wrong. Lines 8–11 use a variety of sound effects and very positive vocabulary to present the initial experience of this escapade. He says the boat left behind her

still, on either side,

Small circles glittering idly in the moon,

Until they melted all into one track

Of sparkling light.

Listen to those lines: Wordsworth uses no figurative language, but there is a preponderance of *s*, *l* and *m* sounds which give a gentle, restful feeling which reinforces the meanings of the words. The lines are given more aural coherence by assonance: *side/idly/light* and by consonance - track/sparkling. Wordsworth has decided to row across the lake and has picked out a craggy ridge as his landmark towards which he is heading.

This positive tone and atmosphere continues up to line 20. The boat is an *elfin pinnace* – playful, mischievous (like an elf) – and the boat moves through the water *like a swan* – a beautiful, majestic bird.

And then the whole tone changes. By a trick of perspective, as Wordsworth rows across the lake, a huge peak comes into view. When you row, you face the direction you started from and the further Wordsworth rows from the shore of the lake, the mountains behind his starting point start to appear and they get larger and larger the more he rows. Look at how the poet describes it and his response to it:

a huge peak, black and huge,

As if with voluntary power instinct,

Upreared its head. I struck and struck again,

And growing still in stature the grim shape

Towered up between me and the stars, and still,

For so it seemed, with purpose of its own

And measured motion like a living thing,

Strode after me.

Like nature, like the boat, the peak is personified and takes on a life of its own, but note also the way a sense of panic in the poet is created by simple repetition of *huge* and *struck*; these lines are full of sibilance too – which creates a sinister, hissing sound. Wordsworth's reaction is one of guilt and shame:

With trembling oars I turned,

And through the silent water stole my way.

He puts the boat back where he found it and then finds he is haunted by this experience for many days afterwards. He does not fully understand what has happened to him:

my brain

Worked with a dim and undetermined sense

Of unknown modes of being.

He is also depressed by the experience:

o'er my thoughts

There hung a darkness, call it solitude

Or blank desertion.

He cannot take his customary pleasure in nature – *No familiar shapes remained* – and his every waking thought and even his sleep is disturbed by

huge and mighty forms that do not live

Like living men, moved slowly through the mind

By day, and were a trouble to my dreams.

How are we to interpret this poem? If some of the language towards the end of the extract seems a little vague, it is because Wordsworth himself – as a small boy – is struggling to make sense of what happened to him.

What is certain is that this experience is a formative one and leads to an epiphany: the poet is made to feel guilty for taking the boat and in that sense it is an important part of Wordsworth's intention – to show that we can learn morality from nature – not just from books or other people. And so nature is presented as beautiful and inspiring, but also frightening if you do something wrong or immoral. The huge and mighty forms that haunt the young boy's mind in the days that follow the incident seem to suggest that there is a divinity in nature, that the natural world (as Wordsworth sees it) is an expression of the existence of God and one which punishes us when we commit immoral acts – like stealing someone else's boat.

We can also see this extract as charting the passage from innocence to experience, from childhood to adulthood. In the first part of the extract Wordsworth is totally in control – of the boat, the situation and his emotions. What he is doing may be wrong but it is clearly enjoyable for a brief period: this can be seen as showing how attractive it is to sin – we are tempted to do wrong because some sins are very attractive and pleasurable. But the sudden appearance of the mountain changes everything and shows the young poet that he is not in control: there is a higher power that watches over us. In simpler terms we might say that the mountain symbolizes his guilty conscience.

Conflict and Power

This extract is remarkable for the power that Nature has over the young Wordsworth. Nature's influence makes him feel guilt for his casual theft of the boat and exerts a moral influence on him lasting for a long time after the incident. The long poem – *The Prelude* (from which this is an extract) – is full of examples of nature's influence on Wordsworth's spiritual and moral development, demonstrating Wordsworth's Pantheism. There is conflict in the poem too: again the conflict centres around the theft of the boat, and it really involves the internal conflict and guilt that Wordsworth feels and which is heightened by Nature and the looming crag that seems to rise up and overpower him. Wordsworth's personification, his animation of Nature greatly aids the impression on the reader.

A Romantic Poem?

This extract is typically Romantic as is the whole of *The Prelude*. The very act of writing a long autobiographical poem suggests that Wordsworth considers himself an exceptional individual with important truths to convey through his poetry. The supreme importance given to nature – in this passage and elsewhere in *The Prelude* – also marks it out as typically romantic, as does Wordsworth's pantheistic notion that Nature is a living force that can inculcate morality.

Why?

This very famous extract:

- shows nature as a moral and spiritual guide.

- explores the psychology of a young boy and his intense feelings of guilt.

- the importance it attaches to Nature make it a typically Romantic poem.

- explores the attractiveness of wrong-doing, but also the effects of a guilty conscience.

- demonstrates a deep love of and respect for nature.

- focuses very closely on the individual and his relationship with nature.

Here is the second poem that we will look at as an unseen, although it is not to do with place:

The Sick Rose – William Blake

O rose, thou art sick!
  The invisible worm,
That flies in the night,
  In the howling storm,

Has found out thy bed   5
  Of crimson joy,
And his dark secret love
  Does thy life destroy

thou – you

thy - your

Who? The voice of the poet, the invisible worm, a rose.

When? In the night during a storm.

Where? Hard to say... in the bed of the rose.

What? Just using what we know from the poem, we can say that an invisible worm discovers the dark secret love of the rose and destroys it during a storm.

It is obvious that this method will not get us very far with this type of poem or, at least, will not get us beyond a superficial interpretation of what it means. Before you read any further, please read my comments below about William Blake's poem 'London', on page 40 because Blake is also the author of 'The Sick Rose'.

What can we say with any certainty about this poem? Its mood is sinister. It is night-time and there is a howling storm. An invisible worm has found out where the rose has its bed and is coming to take its life. *Found out* suggests that the bed needs to be hidden. Paradoxically, although the worm is going to destroy the life of the rose, the worm has a *dark secret love* for the rose: this is now especially disturbing – a love which is dark and secret and which is destructive of life. Not only is it night and, therefore, dark, but the love of the worm is also dark and secret and destructive. We expect love to be a positive emotion which brings good things to our lives.

When faced with this poem many readers want to interpret the poem symbolically – otherwise it becomes a poem about horticulture. The poem is full of words that we associate with love - *rose, bed, joy, love*. In addition, in our culture sending someone roses, especially red roses, is a token of love. But this is a love which has gone wrong and is destructive. Many readers also find the shape of the worm rather phallic – suggestive of the penis. Think of all the types of love which might be considered 'wrong' or destructive. This is the list I came up with, but I am sure you can think of many others:

- Love for someone who does not love you back.

- Love for someone who is already married or in a relationship.

- Love which cannot be expressed.

- Love that transmits disease through unprotected sex.

- Love between two people from different religions.

- Love which is against the law.

- Love which is unwanted by the person you love.

- Love between two people of different class backgrounds.

- Love between two people of the same gender.

- Love or sexual expressions of love which are condemned by the church or by religious doctrine or law.

- Love which is possessive and selfish.

The point of this list is really to show that Blake's power of compression suggests a love that has gone wrong and leaves us to interpret it. To say that 'The Sick Rose' is about any one of the situations listed above would be totally wrong; to say that it suggests them all and encompasses them all, suggests the power of Blake's writing.

Furthermore, if you have read 'London' and its section later in this book and if you remember that the rose is the national symbol of England, then this poem becomes even more than a poem about love gone wrong – it becomes (perhaps) a poem about the state of England and a warning that it will soon be destroyed. You don't have to identify exactly what or who the worm is – the poem does that for you: the worm is destructive and capable of killing – it is a symbol of ALL the things Blake hated in his society. Blake's point is that the rose is sick and is about to be destroyed by sinister, invisible powers.

Finally, if you need any proof of Blake's power to compress meaning, just look at how many words I have used in an attempt to give meaning to his words: Blake uses (including the title) only thirty-seven! This is part of the poem's power and art – that is uses powerful words and imagery from which we can extract a multitude of meanings.

Why? This astonishingly compressed and darkly evocative poem is

• a protest about the England that Blake lived in.

• a protest about the way the church and society saw certain types of love as wrong.

• a warning that love – or what we call love- can be destructive if it is not fulfilled.

• a plea for tolerance and inclusion for those who conventional morality condemns.

Here is another poem in which Place is important:

'Spellbound' – Emily Jane Brontë

The night is darkening round me,
The wild winds coldly blow;
But a tyrant spell has bound me
And I cannot, cannot go.

The giant trees are bending
Their bare boughs weighed with snow.
And the storm is fast descending,
And yet I cannot go.

Clouds beyond clouds above me,

Wastes beyond wastes below;
But nothing drear can move me;
I will not, cannot go.

Context

Emily Brontë (1818 – 1848) was one of the three famous Brontë sisters who lived in the village of Haworth in Yorkshire. They are famous for their writing, but also because they all had tragically short lives, as did their brother Branwell. Emily's poems were first published in 1846 in a volume of poetry along with others by her sisters – Charlotte and Anne. They published under the assumed names of Ellis, Currer and Acton Bell – so readers would not know they were women and not judge their work harshly as a result of knowing their sex. All three sisters went on to publish novels which you may come across in your other reading in English. Emily published *Wuthering Heights* which is an astonishing book. It has been televised and made into several different film versions. Emily adored the wildness and rugged beauty of the Yorkshire moors and this can be seen in *Wuthering Heights* and this poem.

This poem was written in November 1837 when Emily was nineteen. This poem is usually thought of as belonging to Emily's 'Gondal' period; 'Gondal' was an imaginary world created by the Brontë children in which heroes and heroines battled against terrible and desperate situations. The Brontës (including their brother) wrote poems and short stories set in Gondal which are all linked and interwoven with each other. Fannie Ratchford in *Complete Poems of Emily Jane Brontë*, suggests that this poem refers to an earlier incident in the Gondal chronicles when one of the heroines exposes her child to die on the moors in winter. She cannot bear to watch the child die but she cannot tear herself away from the scene.

tyrant – an absolute ruler, an oppressor.

drear – dreary, gloomy, cheerless.

Who? An unidentified narrator – although the context above suggests it is a mother who has abandoned her baby.

When? At the start of the night. The poem is written in the present tense.

Where? Outdoors. The narrator is vulnerable to the storm which is coming. We might also say, given what we know, that the setting is the Yorkshire moors near Haworth.

What? The narrator, despite the awful weather conditions, cannot leave the moors.

Commentary

This poem is written in the first person and the present tense and this gives it an immediacy and vibrancy. The poem begins as night is falling; in the second stanza there is snow on the trees and the storm is coming; in the final stanza the narrator is surrounded by clouds and wastes. The narrator is held by *a tyrant spell*, but there is a progression in her attitude: in the first two stanzas she says she cannot go, but in the final line she expresses defiance – *I will not go* – the act of braving the storm has become a conscious act.

The fact that it is written in the ballad form is important too: it gives it the feel of something old and ancient as well as creating an insistent rhythm. This rhythm is re-enforced by heavy alliteration – *wild winds, bending... bare boughs* – simple repetition – *clouds* and *wastes* and *cannot* – and the consonance on the letter *l* especially in the first stanza, but throughout the poem. The speaker is encompassed by the storm – it is round her, above her and below her: there is no escape. The poem is given an added air of mystery by the *spell* – which like the trees – is personified.

If we accept the context of this poem suggested above – a mother who has abandoned her child on the moors – then this is a poem about the strength of maternal bonds and the fierceness and passion of a mother's love. Even this terrible storm cannot force her away from her baby. In this interpretation the storm may be seen as a pathetic fallacy for her own mental state at the abandonment of her baby.

However, it was published on its own, without any reference to the original setting of Gondal and the poem means something different, we might argue, on its own. In Victorian times women really were second class citizens. Once they married all their property automatically transferred to their husbands; they did not have the vote and would not get it until the 20th century. The Brontë sisters growing up in a genteel, middle class vicar's family would have been protected from the harsh realities of life and would have been expected to excel at needlework, drawing, playing musical instruments, water-colouring, painting. We know that Emily liked to wander around the moors near the family home, even in appalling weather conditions – and this was probably seen as slightly odd behaviour at the time.

So what? You are probably thinking. But if this is true, then 'Spellbound' becomes a poem of great courage and the wilful pursuit of risk and danger. It can be seen as an assertion of Brontë's determination to experience the full energy and force of the storm, to give herself up to elemental forces, to rebel against the protected, insulated life that was expected of middle-class Victorian ladies. Remember the last line which expresses her wilful determination – *I will not go*. This can be seen as a determined cry for independence and freedom – despite the risks that exist from being exposed to the storm.

Why?

This simple ballad powerfully communicates:

- a sense of the power of nature which inspires awe not fear.

- a woman's determined struggle for freedom from the stifling conditions of Victorian middle class existence.

- a sense of courage and resilience even when faced with the most hostile conditions.

- the narrator's sense of isolation.

- the narrator's desire for danger, risk and excitement.

The poems by Wordsworth and Emily Brontë share important features: they both stress the power of nature, and they both connect their own feelings with the place in which the poem is set. Indeed, the two locations – the mountains surrounding Wordsworth's lake and the storm on the moors that Brontë's speaker endures - are both integral to the overall meaning of both poems, however they are interpreted.

Now one last poem on Place before we start to look at the Anthology itself.

The Wild Swans at Coole – W B Yeats

The trees are in their autumn beauty,
The woodland paths are dry,
Under the October twilight the water
Mirrors a still sky;
Upon the brimming water among the stones
Are nine-and-fifty swans.

The nineteenth autumn has come upon me
Since I first made my count;
I saw, before I had well finished,
All suddenly mount
And scatter wheeling in great broken rings
Upon their clamorous wings.

I have looked upon those brilliant creatures,
And now my heart is sore.
All's changed since I, hearing at twilight,

The first time on this shore,
The bell-beat of their wings above my head,
Trod with a lighter tread.

Unwearied still, lover by lover,
They paddle in the cold
Companionable streams or climb the air;
Their hearts have not grown old;
Passion or conquest, wander where they will,
Attend upon them still.

But now they drift on the still water,
Mysterious, beautiful;
Among what rushes will they build,
By what lake's edge or pool
Delight men's eyes when I awake some day
To find they have flown away?

Context

William Butler Yeats (1865 – 1939) lived through a momentous period of Irish history as there were growing calls for independence from Britain, much violence and finally, in 1922, the establishment of the Irish Free State. Yeats was very interested in the pagan roots of Irish culture and ancient Irish myths, as well as the occult and mysticism. In 1898 he met the Irish playwright Lady Augusta Gregory and from then on spent his summers at her home at Coole Park, County Galway – which is the setting for this poem. Yeats once described Coole Park as the most beautiful place on earth. This poem was the title poem in the collection *The Wild Swans at Coole*, published in 1917.

Who? Yeats, his younger self and the swans on the lake. Yeats writes in the first person and the present tense, although he uses the past tense to look backwards and switches to the future tense in the final stanza.

When? October 1916. The poem was dated when it was first published.

Yeats was 51 and still unmarried and childless.

Where? At the lake at Coole Park in Ireland.

What? Yeats watches the swans and thinks about the first time he saw them and reflects on his life.

Commentary

The opening stanza is peaceful and describes the present. It is autumn and evening – there is a sense that things are coming to an end – the year and the day, but it is beautiful to look at. In the second stanza Yeats tells us that he first came to this lake 19 years ago and counted the swans, who rose up and flew away before he had finished. The third stanza starts to reveal the central idea of the poem: when Yeats first saw these swans he was younger and *trod with a lighter tread*; he was full of youthful optimism, but now his heart is *sore*. The swans, by way of contrast, are unchanged – *Their hearts have not grown old,* which implies that Yeats' heart has. He no longer has the energy for *passion* and *conquest* which still come naturally to the swans. The final stanza looks into the future and wonders where the swans will go next. There is certainty that they will delight men's eyes, but there will come a day when Yeats wakes up and the swans have gone.

The poem centres around two contrasts: Yeats as he is now compared with his younger self; and Yeats in contrast with the swans. The beauty and unchanging nature of the swans is emphasised throughout this poem. Compared to humans they have a beauty, power and grace which never changes. They almost become a symbol of the love that Yeats feels he has no energy for at his age and with a series of unsuccessful romances behind him. By contrast the swans are paired, *lover by lover*, but Yeats is alone and lonely. The swans are *brilliant creatures*: their wings are *clamorous*, like a bell-beat. They are *unwearied still; their hearts have not grown old*; they still have the energy for passion or conquest; they are beautiful and mysterious. They are also, as the title points out, *wild* – a word Yeats associated with passion and energy. Note the repetition of the word *still* throughout the poem: this suggests the unchanging nature of the swans and through the idea of stillness, the fact that we cannot tell what lies beneath the beautiful appearance of the lake and the scene: Yeats is deeply troubled and unhappy. The fact that the final stanza ends with a question shows Yeats' uncertainty about the future and his essential pessimism about love and growing old. Yeats has lost his youthful energy and passion. The second stanza expresses well the energy and passion of the swans:

All suddenly mount

And scatter wheeling in great broken rings

Upon their clamorous wings

Here the verbs of motion - *mount, scatter, wheeling* – all suggest an energy which Yeats no longer has. If the swans are a symbol for love then the final sentence imagines a time when there will no love at all in Yeats' life. It is also interesting to note that Yeats was going through a period during which he was producing hardly any poetry, so that his creative block might also influence his mood in this poem.

Why?

This very famous poem has certain key themes:

- it identifies the unchanging energy and beauty of nature.

- it reflects rather sadly on growing old and the lack of power and energy that older people may feel.

- it is a poem that seems to be bidding farewell to love and relationships.

- it uses the swans as a symbol, a symbolic contrast to everything that Yeats is.

- it meditates on human memory and the passing of time: the swans seem not to have changed, but everything about Yeats has changed.

Just like Wordsworth and Rossetti, Yeats uses Place to reflect on his own feelings, but there is a difference: in Wordsworth Nature takes on a moral force which educates the young Wordsworth; in Brontë, as we have seen, the storm takes on symbolic meanings and helps to define the poet's resistance and rebelliousness; Yeats is more interested in the contrast between him and the swans.

Endings

This may seem like an obvious point, one hardly worth drawing attention to, but you have seen from the poems discussed above that the endings of poems are absolutely vital and crucial to their overall effect. In 'The Sick Rose' the final word – *destroy* – carries threat and menace. You will find in many of the poems in the Anthology the ending – the final stanza, the final line, the final sentence, even sometimes the final word – changes what has gone before and forces us to see things differently. So be aware of this as you read and as you revise. When you are writing about poems, the way they end and the emotional conclusion they achieve is a simple way to compare and contrast them. It may not be easy to express what it is exactly that they do achieve, but make sure you write something about the endings, because the endings are often the key to the whole poem. Remember – a poem (like a song) is an emotional journey and the destination, the ending, is part of the overall message, probably its most important part.

PLACE

'To Autumn' – John Keats

Author and Context

John Keats (31 October 1795 – 23 February 1821) was an English Romantic poet. He was one of the main figures of the second generation of Romantic poets along with Lord Byron and Percy Bysshe Shelley, despite his work having been in publication for only four years before his death. Although his poems were not generally well received by critics during his life, his reputation grew after his death, so that by the end of the 19th century, he had become one of the most beloved of all English poets. He had a significant influence on a diverse range of poets and writers, and the Pre-Raphaelite painters.

The poetry of Keats is characterised by sensual imagery, most notably in the series of odes. Today his poems and letters are some of the most popular and most analysed in English literature. Keats suffered from tuberculosis, for which, at the time, there was no cure and as a result, perhaps, many of his poems are tinged with sadness and thoughts of mortality, as well as having a keen eye for the beauties of nature and the pains of unrequited love.

gourd – a large hard-rinded fleshy fruit of the cucumber family – often hollowed out and used as a container.

kernel – the edible part of a nut.

granary – a store house for grain.

winnowing – to separate the edible part of grain from the inedible part (the chaff) – which used to be done by the wind as the chaff is lighter.

hook – a scythe, a cutting implement to harvest the corn.

gleaner – someone who gathers any ears of corn left by the main reaper.

barrèd clouds – clouds arranged to looks like bars in the sky.

sallows – shallows.

Who? The poet writes an Ode to celebrate all the good things autumn and harvest time brings us.

When? In autumn. Keats wrote the poem on September 19th, 1819, after a long walk in the countryside. He wrote to a friend; ' How beautiful the season is now – How fine the air. A temperate sharpness about it. Really, without joking, chaste weather – Dian skies – I never liked stubble fields as much as now – Aye better than the chilly green of the spring. Somehow a stubble plain looks warm – in the same way that some pictures look warm – this struck me much in my Sunday's walk that I composed upon it.'

Where? Locations shift throughout the poem, but the whole poem is set in the countryside.

What? Some poets in some poems see autumn as a precursor of winter, but Keats is concerned to emphasize autumn's richness and the beauty of the harvest.

Commentary

'To Autumn' is an ode split into three stanzas of eleven lines and with a complex rhyme scheme. The first four lines rhyme ABAB and the next seven CDECDDE. An ode is a serious and dignified lyric poem which eulogizes its subject matter: it is a poem of praise and celebration. The rhyme scheme (which is grand and difficult)Keats uses could be said to befit the beauty and seriousness of his subject matter: it is aesthetically pleasing.In the ode Keats personifies Autumn: the first stanza personifies Autumn (and the sun) in a generalized way and this personification is given added force in the second and third verses by use of apostrophe – Keats addresses Autumn directly. Furthermore, Autumn is personified as a woman who, along with the sun, brings the fruits to ripeness.

The opening line of the poem is justly famous and memorable:

Season of mists and mellow fruitfulness

The preponderance of the soft letters – s, f, l and m – give a warm and tender tone to the line. The first stanza presents the early stages of Autumn – the weather is still hot, so much so that the bees 'think warm days will never cease' and the stanza celebrates the growth and sheer plenitude of autumn with all the fruits and nuts swelling as they approach ripeness. In another famous phrase Autumn is described as the

Close bosom-friend of the maturing sun,

Conspiring with him

how to swell and ripen all the fruits in time for the harvest. Everything in the stanza comes to ripeness – the sun, the vines, the apples, the gourds, the nuts – even the hives are 'o'erbrimmed' with honey. The opening stanza is full of words which suggest repleteness and fullness: 'fill all fruit', 'swell', 'plump', 'o'erbrimmed' – as well as the apples bending with the weight of their ripeness.

The second stanza starts by apostrophizing the season (addressing Autumn):

Who have not seen thee oft amid thy store?

In this stanza the ripening process is complete and Keats describes the outcome. The personified Autumn is to be found in a granary surrounded by the harvested grain or asleep in a 'half-reaped furrow'. Autumn also appears as 'a gleaner' and at the end of the stanza is to be found

... by a cider-press, with patient look,

Thou [Autumn] watchest the last oozings, hours by hours.

The second stanza has a sleepy, lazy tone and mood because the harvest has been gathered in and all the hard work has been done. Keats celebrates the sheer bounty of nature with a tone of wonder and intense satisfaction.

The third stanza looks forward to winter and the scene is evening: the poem progresses through time in two ways: the development of autumn and, broadly, the progression through the day. However, Keats starts the stanza in an original way by asking a question:

Where are the songs of Spring? Aye, where are they?

Think not of them — thou hast thy music too.

There are many poems in English which praise the Spring: Keats is arguing that Autumn too deserves praise for its songs and its attractions. Keats paints the beauty of Autumn:

... while barrèd clouds bloom the soft dying day,

And touch the stubble-plains with rosy hue.

But winter is approaching:

... in a wailful choir the small gnats mourn

and the 'light wind lives or dies'. The gnats are mourning because winter will come and they will die. Just as the first verse was full of images of ripeness and fullness, the third verse is full of images of dying — because the end of Autumn is the start of winter — but it is not as simple as that.

On line 30 Keats mentions the 'full grown lambs' but this implies the new-born lambs that the following spring will bring. In the final line Keats writes of the 'gathering swallows' that 'twitter in the skies': they are gathering to make their annual migration, but they will return the following year in late spring. Therefore, while the final stanza contains images of death and precursors of winter, it also contains hints of spring and the seasons' annual cycle of renewal. The poems progress through Autumn and through a single day is complete as the day is 'soft-dying' as the sun sets. This stanza is given added piquancy because Keats suffered from tuberculosis and knew that he would probably die at a relatively young age.

This leads neatly on to the poem's other themes. Keats' poem is at heart a celebration of Autumn and the harvest – the sheer fullness of the harvest and the combined companionship of the sun and the season. Keats presents the harvest in all its glorious plenitude, but the final stanza mentions that winter is on its way. The other great themes of 'Ode to Autumn' are mutability and stability. In the final stanza the swallows are gathering to migrate – winter with its harsh weather is on its way – so the seasons are mutable – they change. But they also represent stability too: the swallows will return next summer and the process of growth to the autumnal harvest will begin again. Reassuringly in one sense the seasons will continue in their natural cycle even after Keats' death.

Keats does not write about one specific named place (unlike many of the poets in the Anthology), but summons up a sense of a generic English landscape at harvest time: specific places are mentioned – the granary, the room with the cider press, the bank on which the tired gleaner dozes – but these have a generic quality and this is surely appropriate because Keats wants to suggest a whole country's harvest coming to fruition at the same time. If there is a single place in Keats' poem, it is the English countryside.

In 'Ode to Autumn' Keats:

- eulogizes the fecundity and plenitude of the English harvest;
- captures the lazy, hazy days of late summer through his word choice;
- brings the harvest and the sun alive through personification;
- introduces more serious themes such as mutability, stability and death and time.

'Composed upon Westminster Bridge, September 3rd, 1802' – William Wordsworth

Author and Context

You can read about Wordsworth on page 24. Here I want to stress how important a city London was in 1802. Although the British Empire was not at its height, London was the capital city of an enormous empire and much of the trade connected with Empire passed through the port of London. It was the biggest city in the world and must have been a truly impressive sight. However, as a poem, it presents a major contrast to William Blake's 'London', the next poem in the Anthology.

garment – article of clothing.

temples – mainly churches and cathedrals, but some synagogues.

Who? The poet as himself writes a sonnet of praise to the city he sees in front of him. (In reality he was accompanied by his sister but she is not mentioned in the poem.)

When? Dawn on September 3rd, 1802.

Where? Halfway across Westminster Bridge.

What? Wordsworth writes a eulogy about the city's magnificence and splendour.

Commentary

'Composed upon Westminster Bridge, September 3rd, 1802' is a Petrarchan sonnet and one of Wordsworth's most famous. Its subject matter is slightly surprising because the vast bulk of Wordsworth's poetry is about nature and the poems are frequently set in the English Lake District, and so the fact that he chose to write a sonnet about London is itself somewhat surprising. He generally sticks to the iambic pentameter, but the first two lines begin with a trochaic foot – an abrupt and arresting start to the poem.

The sonnet is a eulogy to London and its *majesty*:

Earth has not anything to show more fair.

Anyone who can pass by without being impressed is *dull... of soul*. In a simple simile the city is said to wear *the beauty of the morning like a garment* – showing how suited it is to its grandeur and appropriate and natural its majesty is to it. In line 6 the asyndetic list draws attention to the 'official' buildings of London – the buildings which are part of the architectural wonders of the city. The ships remind us that the port of Lonon was the hub of a fast-growing and prosperous empire.The whole scene is arresting and memorable (and a complete contrast to William Blake's 'London'). It is

All bright and glittering in the smokeless air.

In line 9 there is a turn or volta as Wordsworth turns to nature to heap more hyperbolic praise on London. He asserts that

Never did sun more beautifully steep

In his first splendour valley, rock or hill;

Ne'er saw I, never felt, a calm so deep!

The river glideth of his own sweet will!

It is interesting that Wordsworth turns to his habitual subject (nature) in order to better express the marvel and wonder that London presented to Wordsworth on the morning of September 3rd, 1802.

The penultimate line begins with an exclamatory spondee and a wonderful sense of the city about to burst into life:

Dear God! the very houses seem asleep;

And all that mighty heart is lying still.

In this sonnet Wordsworth:

- eulogizes London as the most magnificent sight on earth;
- compares it favourably to natural phenomena;
- is impressed by the power it wields through its institutions;
- likes and enjoys the quietness of the city;
- uses the volta to introduce natural imagery;
- time and place are integral to this poem – even the fact that it is dawn and there is no-one about.

'London' – William Blake

Context and Author

William Blake (1757 – 1827) is now seen as the foremost artist and poet of his time, but his work was largely unknown during his lifetime. He was a painter as well as a poet and you can see some of his paintings in art galleries like Tate Britain in London or the Fitzwilliam Museum in Cambridge. 'London' comes from a collection *Songs of Innocence and of Experience* which appeared together for the first time in 1794. *The Songs of Innocence* (which originally appeared on their own in 1789) are positive in tone and celebrate unspoilt nature, childhood and love. *The Songs of Experience* (from which 'London' comes) depicts a corrupt society in which the prevailing mood is one of despair and in which children are exploited and love is corrupted.

This poem is often read as a profound criticism of the society Blake lived in. Everything in London is owned (*chartered*) - even the River Thames which is a natural force which one might expect to be free. Blake was writing at a time when Britain was the wealthiest country in the world because of its global empire and because of the Industrial Revolution which produced goods which were exported all over the world. But not everyone shared in this enormous wealth; the gap between rich and poor was huge, with the poor suffering really terrible living and working conditions. This poem first 'appeared' (this term will be explained below) in 1794. The date of publication is crucial: Blake is partly seeing London in this way because of events in France. In 1789 the French Revolution began, changing French society forever and ushering in a new age of freedom, equality and brotherhood. Many English people saw what was happening in France and thought it was good to have a society based on greater equality; they looked critically at British society and saw appalling inequalities and injustices. For example, you may be aware that this was the period in British history that some people campaigned against slavery in the British Empire: what is less well-known is that forms of slavery existed in London. There are recorded cases of parents selling their sons to master chimneysweeps in London. The life of a chimney sweep was likely to be short: they were sent up the chimneys of large houses to clean them. Some suffocated; others were trapped in the confined space and died; sometimes their masters would light fires below them to encourage them to work faster – they sometimes were burnt alive. For those who survived, their health was affected: they suffered from terrible lung complaints as a result of breathing in coal dust and, because of poor hygiene, might also succumb to testicular cancer brought on by the accumulated layers of biting coal dust.

Blake had produced *Songs of Innocence* on its own in 1789, although we can tell from his surviving notebooks that he always intended to write *Songs of Experience*. I have used the term 'appeared' because they were not published in a conventional sense. Blake produced each copy of *Songs of Innocence and of Experience* at home by hand and copies were then given to friends and acquaintances. Part of this was Blake's own choice, but we can easily see that his views about Britain and its government would have been highly controversial, so open publication of them may have led to charges of sedition or treason. The British government at the time were terrified of a revolution here, like the one in France, and were doing everything they could to silence people like Blake who were critical of the society in which they lived.

Blake earned his living as an engraver. Before photographs and modern ways of reproducing images, engravings were the cheapest and easiest way of illustrating a book. Blake produced illustrations for other people's books throughout his life – that was how he earned a living. To create an engraving, the engraver has to carve, with a specialist knife, lines on a metal plate; when the plate is then covered in ink and pressed on paper the lines appear on the paper.

Blake used the same technique for reproducing his own poems. After coating the metal plate with ink and producing the outline, Blake coloured each page of each copy of *Songs of Innocence and of Experience* by hand with water colour paint. It is estimated that only 25 copies were produced in his lifetime. If you go to the British Museum you can see one copy: it is tiny and exquisitely detailed and, of course, very personal, because Blake coloured it by hand himself. In addition, to produce his poems in this way was time-consuming and arduous, since in order for the words to appear the right way round when the page was printed, they had to be written in mirror hand-writing on the plate – a painstaking process that must have taken hours and shows not only Blake's artistry, but also his devotion to hard work.

chartered – owned. The charter was a legal document proving possession.

mark – to notice.

marks – signs.

ban – a government edict banning people from doing something.

manacles – handcuffs or leg-irons.

hapless – unlucky.

harlot – prostitute.

marriage hearse – an oxymoron; Blake juxtaposes the idea of death (hearses carry the dead body to the graveyard) with life – marriage often produces children.

Who? The narrator recounts what he sees in the first stanza and in the next three stanzas what he hears as he wanders around London. The poem is written in the present tense which gives it an immediacy and greater impact.

When? 1794.

Where? London.

What? The narrator sees and hears a population suffering and full of pain and despair.

Commentary

The poem's narrator wanders through the streets of London looking at the suffering of his fellow citizens which is apparent on their faces. The first stanza concentrates on what he sees; the second stanza changes to the sounds he can hear and this continues until the end of the poem. Everywhere he goes he sees people who are repressed and downtrodden; in the third stanza he hears the cry of a chimney sweep and the sigh of a soldier; in the final stanza, at night, at midnight, he hears the curse of *the youthful harlot* (very young prostitute) whose *curse* rings out in the night and *blasts* the *marriage-hearse*. We might note that there is no interaction between Blake and the sights and sounds he sees; the only interaction that there is evidence of is the *new-born infant* in the final stanza – the product of a sexual act – but the baby cries and is born into a world of misery and degradation. Nowhere in the poem do we meet a complete human being: we see their marks and hear them, but there is no encounter with any complete human being, suggesting at once their isolation, but also their lack of completeness and community in this horrifying city.

In the first stanza Blake uses simple repetition of the word *chartered* and *marks* (although with a slightly different meaning). The oppression he sees is all-consuming – he sees it in every face he meets. Note the last line which uses parallelism of sound:

Marks of weakness, marks of woe.

The word *mark* is repeated and is then followed by two words which alliterate. This combination of the letter *m* and *w* is very soft and gentle and creates a sense of overwhelming sadness. Note how *mark* starts as a verb in a very innocuous sense and then becomes a repeated noun, suggesting that there is an indelible mark on all the citizens of London.

The second stanza picks up the word *every* and repeats it five times to suggest the situation he is describing is all—encompassing. Again the final line is significant. The manacles that imprison people are *mind-forged* — they are forged, made in the mind. Is Blake suggesting that the people of London are not even aware of their own oppression? Is it something in their mentality, their minds, which prevents them from protesting? Do they have too much faith in their own rulers? Do they not question the system? Note too how Blake delays the verb of the second stanza — *I hear* — until the very last two words of the stanza. Blake's use of repetition in the first two stanzas has another purpose: his language becomes as restricted and limited as the lives of the people he describes. The word *ban* often stirs some debate: you may read elsewhere that it is a reference to the marriage banns — the announcements of a couple's intention to marry. This ties in with the final stanza, but, according to the Oxford English Dictionary, marriage banns have never been spelt with a single *n*. Isn't it more likely that Blake means prohibitions, banning something? Such as public meetings to protest about the condition of the country?

The third stanza continues with the sounds of London: the cry of the chimney sweep and the sigh of the soldier. Why is the church *black'ning*? Some readers suggest that it is a result of pollution caused by industry, but it could be a comment on the moral corruption of the church — it is evil. Why? I think Blake would suggest it is hypocritical: it is appalled by the cry of the chimney sweep, but does nothing to stop slavery. The sibilance in lines 11 and 12 suggest the agony of the soldier. It is an astonishing image — sighs do not run in blood. But the soldier is badly wounded or dying — and he seems to be defending the palace or at least in the pay of the place where the royal family live. Blake uses synecdoche to great effect in this stanza with his use of the words *church* and *palace*: its use here is partly to protect Blake in the repressive society he lived in, but it also serves to distance the establishment and the royal family even further from their subjects.

The worst horrors are saved until the fourth stanza and Blake signals this by stating — *but most* — and what he hears most of all is the curse of the youthful harlot. You can sometimes read that this is a curse in the sense of a bad spell, but it might just as well be a shouted swear word (*curse* had that meaning too). Who she is cursing is unclear, but the curse *blasts the new-born infant's tear.* Perhaps this is an unwanted baby, another mouth to feed, its father one of her clients? The baby is crying and in the final cryptic, oxymoronic line, her curse

blights with plagues the marriage hearse.

The phrase *marriage hearse* is an oxymoron because we normally associate marriage with new life and happiness, whereas we associate hearses with funerals and sadness, so to put the two ideas together is striking and original. Does Blake mean that some marriages are like death? Or that marriage is the death of love? Is marriage something that the youthful harlot will never know? Or is it the marriage of one of her clients? Why do married men visit prostitutes? Some readers even suggest that the curse of the harlot is some sort of sexually transmitted sexual disease which the harlot has given to her client who has then passed it on to his wife – this reading might be supported by the word *plagues*. But *plagues* can be a metaphor too – whatever interpretation you choose, it is wise not to be too dogmatic – the beauty and brilliance of Blake is that he is able to suggest all the above possibilities – and even more.

What is certain is that there is something very wrong with marriage in this final stanza and that the curse of the harlot is frightening and chilling: note Blake's use of harsh plosive consonants in *blasts, blights and plagues* – this is almost onomatopoeic in its presentation of a diseased, corrupt society and Blake's angry reaction to it. We have already mentioned the oxymoron with which the poem ends, but Blake in the third stanza had already juxtaposed things which are not normally associated with each other: the cry of the chimney sweep with the church, and the sigh of the soldier with the palace walls – both these images in a way are oxymoronic. Think back to our comments on 'The Sick Rose' in the introduction – this is a profound and moving criticism of Blake's society.

Finally, Blake's use of the ballad form is important. The ballad form is associated with the oral tradition and with anonymity – it is a more democratic form than the sonnet. However, traditional ballads have a strong narrative drive which this poem lacks. So we can say that Blake takes a form that is popular and egalitarian, and then turns its narrative conventions upside down by writing a poem that is descriptive.

The Final Unpublished Stanza

This is the stanza that was found in Blake's notebooks when he died and which some editions of his complete works publish. As you read it, think about why Blake did not publish this stanza during his lifetime:

Remove away that blackening church;

Remove away that marriage hearse;

Remove away that man of blood —

You'll quite remove the ancient curse!

This makes explicit what is implied in the poem: Blake is calling for a revolution which will *remove* the church and the monarchy: *man of blood* is a phrase famously used by Oliver Cromwell to describe Charles I, the English king who was executed after losing the English Civil War. One can only guess why Blake did not include this stanza, but we can speculate that in 1794 it was too dangerous and that Blake might have got in trouble with the authorities for publishing such a call. Artistically the stanza has its limitations: *remove away* is tautological and, because it makes completely clear Blake's attitude to the things described in the poem as we read it today, one can argue that takes away the cryptic, mysterious quality of Blake's poem as it first appeared. This cryptic nature of the poem encourages us to think and analyze what Blake is saying and thus we are encouraged by the poem to break out of our own *mind-forged manacles*, to expand our minds in order to realize the full impact, the complete implications of what Blake's view of London is. London needs to be changed urgently and by a revolution.

Why?

This very famous poem is remarkable.

- It is a political poem of protest against the authorities.

- This sense of protest makes it an angry and bitter poem.

- Blake speaks up for the marginalized in his society.

- It uses the ballad form in a revolutionary way.

- It is remarkable for its compression of language. Blake manages to pack so much meaning into so few words.

- Its use of simple repetition, sound effects and oxymoronic imagery make it memorable and striking.

'I started Early – Took my Dog' – Emily Dickinson

Author and Context

Emily Elizabeth Dickinson (December 10, 1830 – May 15, 1886) was an American poet. Dickinson was born in Amherst, Massachusetts. Although part of a prominent family with strong ties to its community, Dickinson lived much of her life highly introverted. After studying at the Amherst Academy for seven years in her youth, she briefly attended the Mount Holyoke Female Seminary before returning to her family's house in Amherst. Considered an eccentric by locals, she developed a noted penchant for white clothing and became known for her reluctance to greet guests or, later in life, to even leave her bedroom. Dickinson never married, and most friendships between her and others depended entirely upon correspondence.

While Dickinson was a prolific private poet, fewer than a dozen of her nearly 1,800 poems were published during her lifetime. The work that was published during her lifetime was usually altered significantly by the publishers to fit the conventional poetic rules of the time. Dickinson's poems are unique for the era in which she wrote; they contain short lines, typically lack titles, and often use slant rhyme as well as unconventional capitalization and punctuation. Many of her poems deal with themes of death and immortality, two recurring topics in letters to her friends.

Frigates – sailing ships of medium size.

Hempem Hands – ropes made of hemp.

Bodice – a woman's outer garment covering the waist and bust.

Who? A young woman narrates the poem which is about a visit to the sea.

When? No specific time of day.

Where? By the sea shore and in the local town.

What? A young woman walks to the sea with her dog. She enjoys herself until being intimidated by the force of the waves. She retreats and seeks sanctuary in the town

Commentary

The opening line – *I started Early – Took my Dog* – begins the poem with a sense of light-hearted energy and the fanciful element continues as on her visit to the sea

The Mermaids in the Basement

Came out to look at me.

The metaphor of a house is solid, ordinary and domestic, and is extended with the *Frigates - in the Upper Floor* extend helping hands and ropes. The air of whimsicality is continued by the frigates, the poet writes, *Presuming Me to be a Mouse.*

The third stanza represents a change of tone. It begins with the blunt statement – *But no Man moved Me* – and the Tide rapidly overtakes her, the suddenness of which is reflected in Dickinson's staccato delivery of the lines

...the Tide

Went past my simple Shoe –

And past my Apron – and my Belt

And past my Bodice – too –

Dickinson's use of dashes here is effective in showing the speed with which the tide caught her.

In the next stanza the sea (resolutely masculine) *made as He would eat me up* — but the sense of danger is defused to a large extent by the simile Dickinson uses to present herself:

As wholly as a Dew

Upon a Dandelion's Sleeve —

Dickinson starts and the sea follows:

And then — I started — too —

And He — He followed — close behind —

I felt his Silver Heel

Upon my Ankle — Then my Shoes

Would overflow with Pearl —

In the final stanza Dickinson reaches the safety of the *Solid Town* where the sea seems to know no one and then

…bowing — with a Mighty look —

At me — The Sea withdrew —

The poem is straightforward at a literal level. A young woman walks to the sea with her dog; she enjoys herself until the sea catches her; she becomes frightened and runs to the town for safety. The metaphors of *his Silver Heel* and *Pearl* can be taken to describe a wave breaking and the foam produced.

Most readers would agree that the poem also has a symbolic meaning. Clearly the speaker is initially welcomed by the sea and then attacked and frightened by it. Your reading of the poem will depend on what you feel the sea represents. Readers of the poem generally agree that the sea represents either - sex, the unconscious, death or nature. We will explore the sexual symbolism of the poem.

The speaker is female, timid and innocent, while the sea is male, assertive and aggressive. At the start she is attracted to the sea which is welcoming:

mermaids come and look at her and ships offer help, although they see her as a mouse – a tiny, easily-scared creature.

In stanza three the Sea is personified as a man. The speaker is sexually innocent (*But no Man moved Me*) and felt secure and safe up until this point. But she actually writes that *no Man moved Me – till the Tide* caught up with her and made her wet. The sea engulfs almost her whole body – as high as her bodice and chest. She *started* – is this a frisson of sexual feeling? If we read the poem as sexually symbolic, then his *Silver Heel* and the *Pearl* which overflows her shoes can be seen as the sea's sperm.

On the one hand, the speaker seems to fear the loss of selfhood that sex would entail – she fears that *He would eat me up* – but on the other hand, the rhythm of the verse and the whimsicality of some of the imagery suggest the speaker also finds the whole experience exciting. Her fear may be real, but the safety of the town is easily attainable and at the end of the poem the personified sea bows to her *with a Mighty look* – in a sort of parody of a lover's farewell. Is his look *Mighty* because the speaker acknowledges the power of sexual feeling, despite the fact that she has escaped this time? Or is *Mighty* ironic because the speaker has escaped relatively easily and is now back in the safety of the town? Is her fear, in fact, only light-hearted mock fear?

Emily Dickinson once wrote in a letter: "The shore is safer… but I love to buffet the sea" – a good quotation to summarize the mixture of fear and attraction that is apparent in this poem.

In this short, cryptic poem, Emily Dickinson:

- clearly shows her attraction to a particular place which lies outside the safety of the town;
- describes a potentially frightening experience in a light-hearted and whimsical way;
- uses the sea as a symbol of sex to explore her fears and attractions to sexuality;
- uses language and punctuation in an original and refreshing way.

'Where the Picnic Was' – Thomas Hardy

Author and Context

Author

Thomas Hardy (1840 – 1928) is best known as a novelist. He wrote 15 novels, most of which are set largely in Dorset and the surrounding counties, and which deal with the ordinary lives of ordinary people in stories in which they struggle to find happiness and love – often battling against fate or their own circumstances. His final two novels *Tess of the D'Urbervilles* (1891) and *Jude the Obscure* (1895) both portray sex outside marriage in a sympathetic way and there was such a hysterical public outcry about the novels that Hardy stopped writing fiction and devoted the rest of his life to poetry. Although some of his poetry is intensely personal, this poem is also typical of his work in that it gives a voice to an ordinary man. Although Hardy trained as an architect, he came from a fairly poor family and, in both his novels and his fiction, he never forgets his roots.

An important note. On various internet sources I have read that this poem is about Hardy's dead wife, Emma. There are two reasons why I think this is not the case. The facts of the matter are these: In 1870, while on an architectural mission to restore the parish church of St Juliot in Cornwall, Hardy met and fell in love with Emma Lavinia Gifford, whom he married in 1874. [In 1885 Thomas and his wife moved into Max Gate, a house Hardy had designed himself and his brother had built. Although they later became estranged, her subsequent death in 1912 had a traumatic effect on him and after her death, Hardy made a trip to Cornwall to revisit places linked with their courtship; his *Poems 1912–13* reflect upon her death. In 1914, Hardy married his secretary Florence Emily Dugdale, who was 39 years his junior. However, he remained preoccupied with his first wife's death and tried to overcome his remorse by writing poetry. 'Where the Picnic Was' is NOT included in *Poems 1912 – 13*, suggesting it is not about Emma Hardy. Furthermore, 'Where the Picnic Was' has a time-frame of a single year, yet we know that Hardy's estrangement from Emma lasted many years – again strongly suggesting the poem is not about his dead wife.

sward – green turf, an area of grass.

Who? Hardy – and the three other people who attended the picnic.

When? A year or so after the picnic. In the autumn after the previous year's summer.

Where? On a hill overlooking the sea.

What? Hardy pokes around the remnants of the bonfire they lit at the picnic and reflects on the fate of those who attended the picnic.

Commentary

The first verse contrasts the summer time when *we made the fire, on the hill to the sea* with winter: now Hardy climbs through *winter mire* and the site of the picnic is a *forsaken place*. The identity of *we* is not revealed – this is important for the overall effect of the poem.

The second stanza begins by stressing the wintry weather: *a cold wind blows/And the grass is gray*, but the evidence of the fire they made – the *burnt circle, stick-ends, charred* – are still clearly visible. The end of the second stanza impels us to read on as Hardy admits he is

Last relic of the band

Who came that day!

What has happened to the rest of the band?

The final stanza asserts that Hardy is still there – *Just as last year* – and the sea is the same:

And the sea breathes brine

From its strange, straight line

Up hither, the same

As we four came.

Here the alliteration draws attention to the sea and makes the lines memorable.

The last five lines reveal what has become of the band that had the picnic: two have moved to the city (to the *urban roar/Where no picnics are*). Most poignantly the fourth has died:

… one has shut her eyes

For evermore.

The image of her shutting her eyes forever is a delicate and beautifully tender way of making clear she has died.

Looking back on the poem it can now be seen that the wintry atmosphere (apart from being literal) also acts as a pathetic fallacy representing Hardy's feelings of loss and sadness at the dispersal of the band that had the picnic together. The first two stanzas are both nine lines long and they follow a similar rhyme scheme: ABACBADDC in the first stanza and ABABCCDDB in the second stanza. It could be argued that this lack of regularity reflects Hardy's unease and unhappiness. The final stanza breaks the pattern still further: it is twelve lines long and has the following rhyme scheme: AABBCCDEFDEF. It seems appropriate that the opening of the final stanza should rhyme so simply given Hardy's assertion that he and the sea are unchanged and immutable – the verse reflects this.

And so we have a poem about four friends who went for a picnic one summer day and by autumn of the following year, only one is left: the poet. Two have moved away to try city life and the fourth has died. Place is important in this poem because the place where they had the picnic still shows traces of it, and the sea remains the same, but this is also a poem about the passing of time, the breaking of friendships (through distance) and human mortality. It is a lament about change and the passing of time.

Why?

In this short lyric poem, Hardy:

- expresses his desolate sadness at the death of a friend and the removal of two others associated with a specific place;
- uses pathetic fallacy to represent his feelings of loss;
- expresses mild amazement that he should still be there unchanged;
- venerates the place where the picnic was as the place where all four friends were last together.

'Adlestrop' – Edward Thomas

Author and Context

 Philip Edward Thomas (3 March 1878 – 9 April 1917) was a British poet, essayist, and novelist. He is commonly considered a war poet, although few of his poems deal directly with his war experiences, and his career in poetry only came after he had already been a successful writer and literary critic. Thomas agonized about whether to enlist in the Army, but after months of indecision finally decided to enlist in the army – against the advice of many friends. In 1915, he enlisted in the British Army to fight in the First World War and was killed in action during the Battle of Arras in 1917, soon after he arrived in France. 'Adlestrop' was one of the last poems Thomas ever wrote and he wrote it in the trenches of the Western Front.

Unwontedly – not accustomed to.

No whit less – in the same way, just as.

Who? The poet is on a train which makes an unscheduled stop.

When? We assume that it is set during the First World War.

Where? At a small local railway station at a village called Adlestrop in Gloucestershire. Thomas took the railway trip in June 1914 – before the war – but only wrote about it later as an act of memory.

What? The railway train makes a short, unscheduled stop at a tiny station: no one leaves the train or boards it; Thomas is emotionally overwhelmed by the trees and bushes, and by the sound of bird-song.

Commentary

The poem begins with an affirming *Yes* as if Thomas is speaking to another person or even directly addressing the reader. The poet remembers the tiny village of Adlestrop because one hot afternoon in late June the express train stopped there unexpectedly. He is aware of sounds - the train's *steam hissed* and *someone cleared his throat* – partly because there are no passengers are waiting on the platform and no one leaves the train, so sounds are more easily heard. Through repetition Thomas stresses the fact that the station was completely deserted:

No one left and no one came

On the bare platform.

Perhaps the railway station is so devoid of people because Thomas is writing during the First World War when millions of British men were fighting overseas.

Thomas in the third stanza describes what he remembers of the station at Adlestrop: he saw the name of the station

And willows, willow-herb, and grass,

And meadowsweet, and haycocks dry,

No whit less still and lonely fair

Than the high cloudlets in the sky.

The first two verses had several full stop caesuras which broke up the rhythm and slowed them down. It is significant that here in the third stanza, Thomas avoids such heavy caesuras and uses enjambment too as he writes with enthusiasm about the natural world. His knowledge of the plants he sees proves his enthusiasm for them and for rural England.

The silence on the station is important again in the final stanza:

And for that minute a blackbird sang

Close by, and round him, mistier,

Farther and farther, all the birds

Of Oxfordshire and Gloucestershire.

The silence allows him to hear the blackbird, and to make the imaginative leap to imagine all the birds of two entire counties singing their hearts out in celebration of the weather and the English countryside. In many cultures blackbirds are seen as birds of ill omen – so perhaps the huge chorus of birds is warning of the huge loss of life that will occur (and had already started to occur) when Thomas wrote the poem.

We know that Thomas wrote this poem in the trenches of the Western Front, after he had enlisted as a soldier. I think that must make a difference to the way we read the poem. It is important that the poem is an act of memory as the first line clearly signals – a memory of a beautiful, tranquil day which brings consolation and comfort to a man suffering in the trenches. The natural beauty Thomas describes in the poem might be said to represent the best of the English countryside and acts, therefore, as a beautiful reminder of home and what the soldiers are fighting for. It is typical of Thomas that when he writes a poem about home he chooses to write about a tiny and obscure railway station and the ordinary plants and birds of the English countryside.

Thomas conveys a clear sense of place in this poem and sees the haunting beauty in this obscure Gloucestershire village. His lovingly detailed description of the wild plants and his ability to imagine all the birds of two whole counties joining in song, elevate Adlestrop to the very heights of English pastoral beauty.

In this short but famous poem, Edward Thomas:

- remembers a tiny incident from before the war;
- writes with genuine affection and love about the English countryside;
- perhaps uses the war as background and, therefore contrast to, this picture of a rural idyll;

- perhaps uses this idyllic memory as a consolation to him in the battlefields of France.

'Home Thoughts from Abroad' – Robert Browning

Author and Context

Robert Browning was born in 1812 and became one of the most famous English poets of the Victorian era. He was married to Elizabeth Barrett Browning who was a semi-invalid with an over-protective father. The couple were married in secret and then went to live in Italy. Browning's best work is often set in the past and he was a master of the dramatic monologue, in which the imagined speaker of the poem reveals their innermost thoughts and feelings, often going on to uncover uncomfortable truths about themselves. In this context 'Home Thoughts from Abroad' is not a typical Browning poem because it is largely natural and descriptive.

Who? The poet speaking as himself.

When? In springtime.

Where? Browning lived in Italy but is yearning for England.

What? Browning evokes the joys and pleasures of an English spring from far away in Italy.

Commentary

Browning wrote the poem in 1845 and it was first published in *Dramatic Romances and Lyrics*. On the surface it seems a straightforward poem: living with his family in Italy, Browning is home-sick and nostalgic for an English spring. Spring carries with it connotations of renewal and re-birth after the hiatus of winter – and the promise of new life. In this

Browning owes a lot to the tradition of English Romanticism and its veneration of nature.

The opening stanza has a rhyme scheme, but the line lengths are irregular - perhaps to suggest the joyful frenzy that the thought of England in April causes Browning. It has been suggested by some readers that the rise and fall of lines of different lengths may also suggest his longing for home, along with an acceptance that he cannot return. The poem begins with an exclamation which also suggests his excitement simply at the thought of England in April. Browning is not really being nostalgic: in line three he writes of *whoever wakes in England* – in other words he is imaginatively creating what they will see. Also significant is the tiny detail that Browning writes about are typical of the English spring:

The lowest boughs and the brushwood sheaf

Round the elm-tree bole are in tiny leaf

While the chaffinch sings on the orchard bough.

The final word of the stanza – *now!* – emphasizes his longing to be back home in England.

The second stanza is more regular in its line length and Browning goes on to expatiate on the joys of May in England. The opening of the stanza celebrates the building of nests by birds – the whitethroat and the swallows. There is metrical variation in lines 11, 12 and 13 – each line starting with a trochaic foot which helps to convey enthusiasm and energy – the predominant rhythm in the second stanza being iambic. Browning then imagines his *blossomed pear-tree* scattering *blossoms and dew-drops*. His attention turns to the thrush who

… sings each song twice over

Lest you think he never could recapture

The first fine careless rapture.

With the mention of the fields *rough with hoary dew*, Browning admits that all is not ideal, but the dew will be dissipated when the noontime wakes anew. In short, as the final line admits, Browning yearns for an English spring in contrast to what surrounds him in Italy: the *gaudy melon flower*.

Browning wrote this poem in exile and for British men and women of the Victorian era, exile from Britain was becoming more normal. Of course, very few ended up in Italy like Browning: most were stretched out all over the world as the British Empire continued to grow and needed people to settle it or to run the colonial administration. In the minds of these exiles, Britain, or England as they often called it, came to have the idealized presentation that it does clearly have in Browning's poem.

This short but memorable poem:

- acts as a paean to the English spring;
- includes lovingly-recalled details of England in April and May;
- shows Browning's wider homesickness for his native land;
- presents an idealized picture of an English spring;
- Browning's patriotism extends to the tiny features of rural England – chaffinches, thrushes, swallows – and the blossom on his pear tree coming into bloom.

'First Flight' – U A Fanthorpe

Author and Context

Born in south-east London, the daughter of a barrister, Fanthorpe was educated at St Catherine's School, Bramley in Surrey and at St Anne's College, Oxford, where she received a first-class degree in English language and literature, and subsequently taught English at Cheltenham Ladies' College for sixteen years. She then abandoned teaching for jobs as a secretary, receptionist and hospital clerk in Bristol – in her poems, she later remembered some of the patients for whose records she had been responsible.

Fanthorpe's first volume of poetry, *Side Effects*, was published in 1978. She was "Writer-in-Residence" at St Martin's College, Lancaster (now University of Cumbria) (1983–85), as well as Northern Arts Fellow at Durham and Newcastle Universities. In 1987 Fanthorpe went freelance, giving readings around the country and occasionally abroad. In 1994 she was nominated for the post of Professor of Poetry at Oxford. Her nine collections of poems were published by Peterloo Poets. Her *Collected Poems* was published in 2005. Many of her poems are for two voices. In her readings the other voice is that of Bristol academic and teacher R. V. "Rosie" Bailey, Fanthorpe's life partner of 44 years. The couple co-wrote a collection of poems, *From Me To You: love poems*, that was published in 2007 by Enitharmon. Fanthorpe died, aged 79, on 28 April 2009, in a hospice near her home in Wotton-under-Edge, Gloucestershire.

cumulus – a kind of cloud consisting of rounded heaps with darker bases;

mackerel wigs – 'wigs' makes this a metaphor but the word 'mackerel' refers to a type of cloud cover – so called because it resembles the pattern on the skin of a mackerel.

Who? The poet as herself and (in italicized speech) a selection of her fellow travellers.

When? In daylight towards sunset.

Where? On an aeroplane – it is Fanthorpe's first flight. She describes the view of the clouds from 28,000 feet.

What? There is a consistent contrast between the banal and clichéd reactions of the other travellers (printed in italics) and the more nuanced and perceptive reactions of the main speaker. Meanwhile, Fanthorpe is entranced by the view from the aeroplane, particularly in its position above the clouds.

Commentary

This poem details Fanthorpe's first flight in an aeroplane – and she readily admits that she doesn't *like the feel of it*. The poem also consists of two voices: Fanthorpe's own voice, open to the beauty of the world above the clouds and also, in italics, the words said by seasoned travellers – almost all banal clichés and truisms. These interjections in italics serve as a contrast with Fanthorpe's more innocent, more open sense of wonder. The two voices always occur in different stanzas, so visually the poem is easy to follow.

Fanthorpe describes take off:

A sudden swiftness, earth slithers

Off at angle.

The more experienced travellers exchange small talk (*This is rather a short hop for me*, read newspapers and discuss secretaries), but Fanthorpe is excited now and cranes to see through a window to look at England below. She sees

Familiar England, motorways, reservoir,

Building sites.

All the time Fanthorpe is reminding us of the other passengers' reactions - rather mundane compared with Fanthorpe's enthusiasm: *I'm doing it just to say I've done it, Tell us when we get to water, The next lot of water'll be the Med.*

Once they are above the clouds Fanthorpe uses a striking metaphor to describe the cloud and the effect of the sun shining on it:

Under us the broad meringue kingdom

Of cumulus, bearing the crinkled tangerine stain

That light spreads on an evening sea at home.

Once again Fanthorpe's thoughts are interrupted by a fellow passenger's words:

You don't need an overcoat, but

It's the sort of place where you need

A pullover. Know what I mean?

Theses interjections contrast the banal reality of air travel with Fanthorpe's thoughts and impressions, but they also keep the poem grounded in a reality that the reader is likely to recognize.

Fanthorpe expresses great excitement at the freedom air travel brings, She writes:

We have come too high for history.

Where we are now deals only with tomorrow,

Confounds the forecasters, dismisses clocks.

They have come too high for history as no history has been made at such a height and their thoughts are on the future, on the trips they are making. The weather forecasters are confounded because the plane is above the cloud line and the forecasters deal with weather at ground level. Now they are in flight all that matters is their destination and clocks have been dismissed as they are travelling through different time zones – so there is no fixed time on the aeroplane.

Fanthorpe conveys a sense of awe and excitement at her first flight. The poem ends with an intriguing paradox:

Mackerel wigs dispense the justice of air.

At this height nothing lives. Too cold. Too near the sun.

The mackerel wigs are a common cloud pattern. The poem ends with a seeming paradox: nothing lives at this height, because it's too cold, yet ironically it is closer to the sun and should logically be hotter... if one did not take into account they are flying at 28,000 feet.

Altogether an engaging poem about the excitements of a first flight. Fanthorpe mixes well the comments of her fellow travellers with her own more excited and more interesting account of the flight.

In 'First Flight' U A Fanthorpe

- captures the thrill and excitement of one's first flight;
- finds beauty above the cloud line;
- accurately imitates the inane things that most people say.

'Stewart Island' – Fleur Adcock

Author and Context

Fleur Adcock was born in Auckland, but spent the years between 1939 and 1947 in the UK. Her father was Cyril John Adcock, her sister is the novelist Marilyn Duckworth. Fleur Adcock studied Classics at Victoria University of Wellington, graduating with an MA. She worked as an assistant lecturer and later an assistant librarian at the University of Otago in Dunedin until 1962. She was married to two famous New Zealand literary personalities. In 1952 she married Alistair Campbell (divorced 1958). Then in 1962 she married Barry Crump, divorcing in 1963.

In 1963, Adcock returned to England and took up a post as an assistant librarian at the Foreign and Commonwealth Office in London until 1979. Since then she has been a freelance writer, living in East Finchley, north London. She has held several literary fellowships, including the Northern Arts Literary Fellowship in Newcastle upon Tyne and Durham in 1979–81.

Adcock's poetry is typically concerned with themes of place, human relationships and everyday activities, but frequently with a dark twist given to the mundane events she writes about. Formerly, her early work was influenced by her training as a classicist but her more recent work is looser in structure and more concerned with the world of the unconscious mind.

Stewart Island - (officially named Stewart Island/Rakiura) is the third-largest island of New Zealand. It lies 30 kilometres (19 miles) south of the South Island, across the Foveaux Strait. Its permanent population is 381 people as of the 2013 census, most of whom live in the settlement of Oban on the eastern side of the island. It is inhospitable and very sparsely populated.

Who? The poet appears to speak as herself in this poem.

When? No specific time.

Where? Stewart Island, New Zealand.

What? The poet writes rather critically of Stewart Island which makes the final sentence a logical conclusion to the poem.

Commentary

Fleur Adcock does not like Stewart Island and makes it clear throughout this short but biting poem.

The first stanza begins with the local hotel manager's wife saying 'But look at all this beauty' but, significantly, she has been asked 'how she could bear to/live there' and in the third stanza Adcock sardonically notes that the hotel manager's wife 'ran off' with a Maori fisherman 'that autumn' – abandoning her husband and 'all this beauty'.

In the first stanza Adcock grudgingly admits

True; there was a fine bay,

all hills and atmosphere; white

sand and bush down to the sea's edge.

There is something dismissive about the phrase 'all hills and atmosphere' – Adcock cares so little for Stewart Island that she cannot be bothered to describe or give details of the atmosphere, but just dismisses it with that general word which tells us nothing of the sort of atmosphere it was.

However, the second half of the poem is more critical of Stewart Island: the poet 'walked on the beach', but only because it was too cold to swim; her seven-year-old collects shells 'but was bitten by sandflies'; and her 'four-year-old paddled' until

a mad seagull jetted down

to jab its claws and beak into

his head.

Overall, then, we get the impression of a place which is wild and beautiful, but lacks the trappings of civilization and which is positively antagonistic to human beings. The sandflies and the mad seagull present Adcock's view that this place is hostile to human beings and she is naturally, as any parent would be, protective of her children. The final sentence of the poem, therefore, comes as no surprise, although it is expressed in a weary tone of the inevitable:

...I had already

decided to leave the country.

Biographical context is important here: disliking the raw nature of Stewart Island, Adcock has chosen to live and work for most of her life in London - a bustling metropolis free of sandflies and mad seagulls. In many ways this is an unusual poem because poets often write poems in praise of unspoilt nature – unspoilt by human beings and the things they bring with them. We are especially aware of green or environmental concerns and how human activity can damage the natural environment, and so seek comfort in nature which is unharmed or untouched by human activity. Therefore, Adcock's poem is original in selecting the unpleasant parts of nature and pointing out the uncivilized parts of Stewart Island. Her final sentence too is dismissive in its brevity and simplicity – as if it is a foregone conclusion that she will leave New Zealand and its unspoilt nature. I find this poem quite comical given our current obsession with holidays in 'wild' nature – this is what wild nature is really like!

In this poem Fleur Adcock makes clear

- her detestation of wild nature and Stewart Island in particular;
- her dislike of the uncivilized parts of New Zealand;
- her disdain for the cultural emptiness of Stewart Island;
- her determination to leave New Zealand.

'Presents from my Aunts in Pakistan' – Moniza Alvi

Author and Context

Moniza Alvi was born in Lahore, Pakistan. She was born to a Pakistani father and a British mother. Her father moved to Hatfield, Hertfordshire in England when she was a few months old. She did not revisit Pakistan until after the publication of one of her first books of poems - *The Country at My Arm*. She worked for several years as a high school teacher, but is now a freelance writer and tutor, living in Norfolk. She and her husband, Robert, have one daughter. Alvi says: "Presents from My Aunts...was one of the first poems I wrote. When I wrote this poem I wasn't actually back in Pakistan. The girl in the poem would be me at about 13. The clothes seem to stick to her in an uncomfortable way, a bit like a kind of false skin, and she thinks things aren't straightforward for her. I found it was important to write the Pakistan poems because I was getting in touch with my background. And maybe there's a bit of a message behind the poems about something I went through, that I want to maybe open a few doors if possible."

salwar kameez – a long tunic worn over a pair of baggy trousers.

sari – a long cloth wrapped around the waist and covering the shoulder, neck and head.

filigree – ornamental metallic lacework of silver or gold.

prickly heat – a skin disease, inflammation of the sweat glands with intense irritation.

the Shalimar Gardens – a beautiful complex of gardens, fountains and trees in Lahore, Pakistan.

Who? The poet speaks as herself – a woman of Pakistani origin growing up in the UK.

When? The poem focuses on her childhood and teenage years at about the age of 13.

Where? The poem is set in the UK but there are frequent references to Pakistan.

What? Much of the poem discusses the clothes that the speaker was sent by relatives in Pakistan and the speaker's desire to wear Western clothes and, therefore, to fit in with British society.

Commentary

One of the first things one notices about this poem is the way it is set out with lines beginning half way across the page. The reason for this, as will become clear in the commentary, is that Alvi is torn between her ethnic heritage in Pakistan (shown in the illustration of the salwar kameez) and her upbringing in the UK. The seeming confusion on the page represents the two conflicting forces playing on the young Alvi and her own confusion about where she belongs. In this sense, the lay out of the poem is entirely appropriate and enhances the meaning of the words. The left and right hand side of the page represent her English growing up and her Pakistani heritage. She is torn between the two just as the words move from side to side.

Moniza Alvi contrasts the exotic and beautiful clothes sent to her by her aunts in Pakistan with what she sees around her in Britain. She has two problems with the gifts: firstly, they seem too beautiful, too exquisite for her to wear; secondly, they seem out of place in modern Britain. Many of the lines are centralized, showing how she is caught in the middle between two cultures. The salwar kameez are brightly coloured and exotic –

peacock-blue

and another

glistening like a split orange.

They send bangles and an apple-green sari bordered in silver for her teens.

Alvi tried the clothes on but felt *alien in the sitting room -*

I could never be as lovely

> *as those clothes.*

In fact, Alvi admits *I longed for denim and corduroy*. She describes her salwar kameez as her *costume* which suggests it is not ordinary clothing, but more a theatrical costume she wears when she is playing at being Pakistani — but the problem is she is half-English. She writes

My costume clung to me

> *and I was aflame,*

I couldn't rise up out of its fire,

> *half-English,*

> *unlike Aunt Jamila.*

The image of her being *aflame* (because of the beautiful colours) is a striking metaphor because it shows how distraught she is about her cultural identity.

She turns on the camel-skin lamp in her bedroom

to consider the cruelty

> *and the transformation*

from camel to shade.

She is appalled by the cruelty involved, but is still able to

> *marvel at the colours*

like stained glass. —

once again showing her ambivalence to her mixed identity.

We are told in the fourth stanza hat her mother cherishes her jewellery, but that it was stolen from their car. The presents from her aunts were *radiant* in her wardrobe — suggesting that that is where they stayed and that she never wore them. In return, somewhat ironically, the aunts in Pakistan request to be sent cardigans from Marks and Spencer.

Alvi's eastern clothes did not impress the school friend she showed them to, but she herself used to admire the mirror work and it prompted memories of how her mother, her father and Alvi had first travelled to England. She sees herself in the miniature glass circles — and because the mirrors are tiny she sees multiple images of herself — again suggesting the fragmentary sense of self that Alvi has.

She never visited Pakistan but pictured it from 1950s photographs and, as she got older, became aware of it on the news — *conflict, a fractured land. Throbbing through newsprint.* Sometimes she imagined Lahore and her aunts

screened from male visitors,

> *sorting presents,*

> *wrapping them in tissue.*

At the end of the poem she pictures other scenes from Lahore:

Or there were beggars, sweeper girls

> *and I was there — of no fixed nationality,*

staring through the fretwork

> *at the Shalimar Gardens.*

Alvi imagines other destinies for herself, had she not emigrated to England with her mother and father. Of course, she would be staring at the fretwork of the Shalimar Gardens because a beggar girl would not be allowed in. the poem ends on a note of poignant sadness: Alvi still feels of *no fixed nationality.*

This poem expresses well the problems that people with diverse cultural backgrounds have. It is good to compare this poem with 'Hurricane Hits England' – which has a very different ending.

In this poem Alvi

- demonstrates the pressures that those from dual cultural heritages have to suffer;
- gives a fascinating insight into British Pakistani home life;
- fails to resolve the problems of duality;
- reminds us of the richness of Pakistani culture and mores.

'Hurricane Hits England' – Grace Nichols

Author and Context

Grace Nichols was born on the Caribbean territory of Guyana in 1950. Since 1977 she has lived in Britain with her partner, John Agard. They are both poets. Although she lives in the UK, she is very aware of her past and the traditions of Guyana, and many of her poems explore the clash or conflict between British or European values and those of her West Indian and African ancestors or, as this one does, they celebrate her African heritage, contrasting it with life in the UK. Nichols herself has said:

I am a writer across two worlds; I just can't forget my Caribbean culture and past, so there's this constant interaction between the two worlds: Britain and the Caribbean.

These two worlds are contrasted and juxtaposed in this poem.

'Hurricane Hits England' - The Great Storm of 1987 was a violent extratropical cyclone that occurred on the night of 15–16 October, with hurricane-force winds causing casualties in England, France and the Channel Islands as a severe depression in the Bay of Biscay moved northeast. Among the most damaged areas were Greater London, the East Anglian coast, the Home Counties, the west of Brittany and the Cotentin Peninsula of Normandy which weathered gusts typically with a return period of 1 in 200 years.

Forests, parks, roads and railways were strewn with fallen trees, and the British National Grid suffered heavy damage, leaving thousands without power. At least 22 people were killed in England and France. The highest measured gust of 117 kn (217 km/h; 135 mph) was recorded at Pointe Du Roc, Granville, France and the highest gust in the U.K. of 100 kn (190 km/h; 120 mph) was recorded at Shoreham-by-Sea.

That day's weather reports had failed to indicate a storm of such severity, an earlier, correct forecast having been negated by later projections. The storm remains famous because of the damage it caused; because it was not forecast; and because hurricanes do not normally occur in the United Kingdom.

howling ship – perhaps an allusion to the original ships which brought African slaves to the Caribbean and the Americas.

Huracan – the Carib god of the hurricane.

Oya – goddess of the Niger river in Africa.

Shango – Caribbean god of thunder and lightning.

Hattie – name of a Caribbean hurricane.

Who? The poem is a third person narrative about an unnamed woman of Caribbean descent living in the UK, but switches to the first person.

When? 1987. The southern counties of England were hit by hurricane-force winds: many trees were uprooted and lots of buildings were damaged.

Where? Mainly along the South Coast of England and in the Home Counties.

What? Grace Nichols herself has said: 'Because I'd never associated hurricanes with England (a regular Caribbean phenomenon) the manifestation of one in England took on a deep significance for me. It was as if some invisible but potent connection has taken place between the two landscapes. As if the voice of the old gods from Africa and the Caribbean were in the winds of the hurricane as it raged around Sussex.' This is a key quotation and informs the first half of the poem.

Commentary

Nichols uses the occasion of the Great Storm to link two places that are close to her heart – England and Guyana. The opening litany of original Carib gods and ones brought by the slaves to the New World serves as a litany which melds the two cultures together and brings the Caribbean to England – just as the two cultures are blended in Nichols herself. The Great Storm has come to England but England is not prepared for the Great Storm. The Caribs were the original inhabitants of the region – all killed in war or died because of a lack of immunity to European diseases.

In the opening stanza (written in the third person) we are told

It took a hurricane, to bring her closer

To the landscape.

The hurricane keeps her awake half the night and it is frightening – we hear of its *gathering rage*. There is also an allusion to the slave trade – *the howling ship of the wind* – the original ships used to transport Africans to the Americas to act as slaves – a tragic episode in human history. The final line of the first stanza describes the storm as *Fearful and reassuring*. This oxymoron conveys the fear of the storm, but also that the hurricane reminds the young woman of home in the Caribbean – and is, therefore, reassuring.

In the second stanza the speaker appeals to the ancient Carib and African gods to talk to her and refers to Hattie as My sweeping, back-home cousin – which clearly shows her closeness to her Caribbean roots and an element of nostalgia.

The speaker in the third stanza is perplexed and confused:

Tell me why you visit,

An English coast?

What is the meaning

Of old tongues

Reaping havoc

In new places?

The lightening in the fourth stanza is a blinding illumination which disrupts the electricity supply and forces them into *further darkness.*

The speaker remains confused and perplexed in the fifth stanza and gives a vivid idea of the destructiveness of the storm with trees

Falling heavy as whales

Their crusted roots

Their cratered graves?

The speaker is still searching for meaning in the hurricane and its ferocity. 'Whales' is an interesting simile – chosen no just because of the comparison with size, but also because it is a huge ocean-going mammal and this fits in the other imagery to do with the sea. 'Roots' can also be linked with the speaker's roots which are crusted – suggesting they are in need of renewal.

The arrival of the hurricane which she associates with home in the Caribbean, the speaker says, has *unchained [her] heart.* Grace Nichols has written that it is "as if the hurricane has broken down all barriers between her and the English landscape." She is at last able to reconcile her two cultural tradition – the Caribbean and the English.

The speaker asserts that she is aligning herself to the goddess Oya:

Tropical Oya of the Weather,

I am aligning myself to you,

I am following the movement of your winds,

I am riding the mystery of your storm.

Oya, the speaker says, has come to break the frozen lake in me – to unite her Caribbean and English selves. Grace Nichols has remarked of the ending of the poem:

"In some mysterious way, it seems as if the old gods have not deserted her completely, connecting her both to the Caribbean and to England which is now her home. Indeed to the wider planet as she asserts

the earth is the earth is the earth."

In this poem, Grace Nichols:

- makes clear the devastating power of the Great Storm;
- uses it as a way of summoning old Caribbean and African gods;
- summons up the past historical wrong of slavery;
- uses the storm to allow the speaker to feel at home in England and reconciled to living in two cultural traditions;
- allows the speaker to be perplexed and confused, but to feel joyful and liberated at the end of the poem;
- *the earth is the earth is the earth* – expresses our common humanity and the unity of the world.

'Nothing's Changed' – Tatamkhulu Afrika

Author and Context

Tatamkhulu Afrika was born in 1920 and lived in Cape Town's District Six, which was then a flourishing mixed-race community. People of many different racial backgrounds lived there harmoniously and Afrika claimed that he felt at home there. In 1948 the South African government brought in the apartheid system, based on segregating the races rigidly and denying black South Africans and what the white government called 'coloureds' (people of mixed race and Asian backgrounds) citizenship and the vote. Inevitably non-whites had the least education, the worst jobs and the worst pay. It was a thoroughly iniquitous system, and caused international protests and sanctions, and riots and protests on the streets of South Africa.

During the 1960s, the government designated District Six a 'whites-only' area and evacuated the population. It bulldozed the entire area, much of which remains unbuilt on.

Tatamkhulu was brought up as a white South African, but discovered in his teens that he was the child of an Arabian father and a Turkish mother. He turned down the chance to be classified as white, converted to Islam and was classified by the government as 'coloured'.

The African National Congress (the ANC) was a political and terrorist organization fighting the injustice of apartheid. In 1984 Afrika joined the ANC but was arrested in 1987 on terrorism charges and was banned from writing or speaking in public for five years. He changed his name to Tatamkhulu – which had been his ANC code name. He was able to carry on writing despite the ban.

Afrika has said:

"I am completely African. I am a citizen of Africa – that is my culture. I know I write poems that sound European, because I was brought up in school to do that, but, if you look at my poems carefully, you will find that all of them, I think, have an African flavour".

In 1990 Nelson Mandela, the imprisoned leader of the ANC, was released from prison and the apartheid laws were repealed, but most count 1994 as the real end of apartheid when all South Africans – regardless of skin colour or ethnic background – were allowed to vote in national elections.

Afrika wrote this poem when it was clear that political change was coming to South Africa, and it expresses pessimism for the continuing economic and financial gulf between blacks and whites – something that may take decades to change.

linen fall – the linen table cloths that cover the tables in the new expensive restaurant.

Port Jackson trees – trees imported from Australia.

bunny chow – bread stuffed with sardines or pilchards. A cheap and unsophisticated dish.

Who? The poet returns to the scene of District Six and notes the disparity between an expensive restaurant and a cheap café.

When? In the post-apartheid era.

Where? In Cape Town, South Africa.

What? The poet reflects on the demolition of District Six and his feelings about it. He reflects on the new South Africa and concludes that *nothing's changed* – the blacks and any other non-whites are still mired in poverty and economically excluded from certain places.

Commentary

The poem is written in free verse – a frequent choice for poets writing outside the mainstream. To choose a traditional form would be submitting to the prevailing traditional white culture, so free verse signals their independence from that culture and their rebellion against it. Despite being in free verse, on the page the poem consists of six stanzas, all made up of six short lines, which gives it a visual coherence: Afrika is in control of his material and knows precisely what he wants to express, and this is reflected in its regular appearance on the page.

The entire poem is written in the present tense which gives it a vibrant immediacy and a sense of authenticity. Although the poem is based on Afrika's memory of District Six, the poem is set in the present. The opening stanza immediately immerses the reader in the poet's sensibility as he walks on the land which was once District Six – his home before it was bulldozed. The site is derelict and uncared for:

Small round hard stones click

under my heels

...cans

trodden on, crunch

in tall, purple-flowering,

amiable weeds.

The second stanza makes clear that although there is no sign that says the area was once District Six, Afrika lived there for so long that he recognizes it:

...my feet know,

and my hands,

and the skin about my bones,

and the soft labouring of my lungs,

and the hot, white, inwards turning

anger of my eyes.

The reader has to wait until the third stanza to know what has provoked his anger: a *new, up-market, haute cuisine* restaurant has opened, *brash with glass* and *a guard at the gatepost.* Afrika calls it a *whites-only inn,* but admits there is no sign while ruefully admitting *we know where we belong.* The poet presses his nose to the windows of the restaurant knowing he will see a luxurious interior with *crushed ice white glass,* immaculate table linen and a rose on each table.

The fifth stanza presents a contrast:

Down the road,

working man's café sells

bunny chows

The tables are made of plastic, there are no napkins (you wipe your fingers on your jeans) and people spit on the floor. Afrika explains – *It's in the bone* – it is what people are accustomed to. The mass of South Africans – the black and Asian and mixed race South Africans are excluded from the posh new restaurant by a lack of money and by social habit.

In the final stanza he backs away from the glass. What he has seen moves him to passionate, violent anger:

Hands burn

for a stone, a bomb

to shiver down the glass.

And he comes to the conclusion that forms the title of the poem: *Nothing's changed.* The political system has changed and true democracy has arrived in South Africa, but there is still a yawning economic gulf between whites and non-whites in the country.

Tatamkhulu wrote about the poem:

'Nothing's Changed' is entirely autobiographical. I can't quite remember when I wrote this, but I think it must have been about 1990. District Six was a complete waste by then, and I hadn't been passing through it for a long time. But nothing has changed. Not only District Six…. I mean, we may have a new constitution, we may have on the face of it a beautiful democracy, but the racism in this country is absolutely redolent. We try to pretend to the world that it does not exist, but it most certainly does, all day long, every day, shocking and saddening and terrible. Look, I don't want to sound like a prophet of doom, because I don't feel like that at all. I am full of hope. But I won't see it in my lifetime. It's going to take a long time. I mean, in America it's taken all this time and it's still not gone… so it will change. But not quickly, not quickly at all.

'Nothing's Changed' by Tatamkhulu Afrika

- evokes a clear sense of different, contrasting places;
- clearly conveys an angry bitterness about the new restaurant and wants to destroy it;
- adds a political dimension to his description of place;
- makes clear his political views regarding the new South Africa — both during the Apartheid era and the post-Apartheid era.

'Postcard from a Travel Snob' – Sophie Hannah

Author and Context

Sophie Hannah was born in Manchester, England; her father was the academic Norman Geras and her mother is the author Adèle Geras. She attended Beaver Road Primary School in Didsbury and the University of Manchester. She published her first book of poems, *The Hero and the Girl Next Door*, at the age of 24. Her style is often compared to the light verse of Wendy Cope and the surrealism of Lewis Carroll. Her poems' subjects tend toward the personal, utilizing classic rhyme schemes with understated wit, humour and warmth. She has published five previous collections of poetry with Carcanet Press. In 2004, she was named one of the Poetry Book Society's Next Generation poets.

Hannah is also the author of a book for children and several psychological crime novels. Her first novel, *Little Face,* was published in 2006 and has sold more than 100,000 copies. Her fifth crime novel, *Lasting Damage,* was published in the UK on 17 February 2011. *Kind of Cruel*, her seventh psychological thriller to feature the characters Simon Waterhouse and Charlie Zailer, was published in 2012.

Her 2008 novel *The Point of Rescue* was produced for TV as the two-part drama *Case Sensitive* and shown on 2 and 3 May 2011 on the UK's ITV network. It stars Olivia Williams in the lead role of DS Charlie Zailer and Darren Boyd as DC Simon Waterhouse. Its first showing had 5.4 million viewers. A second two-part story based on *The Other Half Lives* was shown on 12 and 13 July 2012.

In 2013, Sophie's novel, *The Carrier*, won the Crime Thriller of the Year Award at the Specsavers National Book Awards. Two of Sophie's crime novels, *The Point of Rescue* and *The Other Half Lives*, have been adapted for television and appeared on ITV1 under the series title Case Sensitive in 2011 and 2012. In 2004, Sophie won first prize in the Daphne Du Maurier Festival Short Story Competition for her suspense story *The Octopus Nest*, which is now published in her first collection of short stories, *The Fantastic Book of Everybody's Secrets*. Sophie has also published five collections of poetry. Her fifth, *Pessimism for Beginners*, was shortlisted for the 2007 T S Eliot Award. Her poetry is studied at GCSE, A-level and degree level across the UK. From 1997 to 1999 she was Fellow Commoner in Creative Arts at Trinity College, Cambridge, and between 1999 and 2001 she was a fellow of Wolfson College, Oxford. She lives with her husband, children and dog in Cambridge, where she is a Fellow Commoner at Lucy Cavendish College.

philistine – a person indifferent or hostile to culture.

connoisseur – a well-informed judge of, for example, wine or food.

Who? The speaker is a person who despises ordinary British tourists who go abroad for good weather and cheap alcohol.

When? No specific time of day but the poem is set in the present.

Where? Nowhere specific, but various general foreign locations are evoked. Two types of foreign holiday resort are evoked: one which caters for British people who just go abroad for good weather and cheap alcohol and who are not interested in the local culture; the other type of location is that preferred by the speaker, the travel snob – which offers a supposedly authentic holiday experience.

What? The 'travel snob' derides the behaviour and activities of the average British tourist, and, in so doing, comes across as arrogant and self-satisfied.

Commentary

In many ways this is a satiric poem, but as we shall see by the end of this commentary both ordinary holidaymakers and the speaker of the poem are being satirized.

Millions of Britons take overseas holidays each year. The vast majority go to hot, sunny places to escape the miserable and changeable English weather: they go to resorts packed with other foreign tourists where the food and the alcohol are cheap and plentiful. One gets the sense that such holiday makers do not care which country they go to as long as the sun shines and the alcohol is cheap: they appear to have no interest in the local culture and history.

In the last few years there has risen a trend where more discerning tourists seek out less well-known holiday destinations in order to avoid the typical British holidaymaker and attempt to enjoy – unadulterated – the local culture. This poem is about these different types of holiday maker. The speaker is a more discerning holiday maker who denigrates those who travel to recognized holiday resorts.

In the first stanza the speaker, the travel snob, glories in her isolation from ordinary holiday resorts and pours scorn on conventional holiday resorts

with karaoke nights and pints of beer

for drunken tourist types – perish the thought.

The speaker takes pride in their isolation

I do not wish that anyone were here

and

This place is not a holiday resort.

In the second stanza the speaker derides 'your seaside-town-consumer-hell' and glories in the authenticity of her holiday – she's sleeping in a 'local farmer's van' miles away from guest houses and hotels.

The speaker returns to the difference between her and the average British tourist in stanza three:

I'm not your sun-and-sangria-two weeks-

Small-minded-package-philistine-abroad.

The speaker is highly critical of ordinary tourists who go abroad and get drunk and behave appallingly, while soaking up the sun and having no interest in the local culture. But this raises important questions: can the travel snob experience the real culture and life of a place? After all, she is a tourist too – albeit a richer, more discerning one.

However, the final stanza turns the tables on the travel snob. The travel snob declares themselves to be 'multicultural' and claims that their friends are 'wine connoisseurs, not drunks' – although the words are very different, it is still possible for a wine connoisseur to get drunk. The final two lines of the poem clinch the double satire that is going on in this poem:

I'm not a British tourist in the sea;

I am an anthropologist in trunks.

That final phrase – 'an anthropologist in trunks' – is so pretentious and pompous that the speaker becomes part of the satire.

This is a very interesting poem: the speaker mounts a sustained attack on the average British tourist's obsession with sun, booze and karaoke – but it is all presented with no warmth, no compassion, no understanding. The speaker himself (I think it is male because of the trunks in the last line) is a pretentious snob – precious, opinionated and derogatory to his fellow human beings. Overall the poem is amusing because it manages to satirise two very different groups of tourists – one through his own words!

Why?

This highly amusing poem:

- satirizes the conventional British tourist interested in cheap booze and sunshine;
- also satirizes the speaker of the poem for his/her pretentiousness and his/her derogatory attitude to the other type of tourist;
- achieves its object succinctly and with humour.

'In Romney Marsh' – John Davidson

Author and Context

John Davidson (11 April 1857 – 23 March 1909) was a Scottish poet, playwright and novelist, best known for his ballads. He also did translations from French and German. In 1909, financial difficulties, as well as physical and mental health problems, led to his suicide.

Romney Marsh is an inhospitable and sparsely populated unspoilt wetland area situated in the counties of Kent and East Sussex in the south-east of England. It covers about 100 square miles (260 km²) and it is very flat.

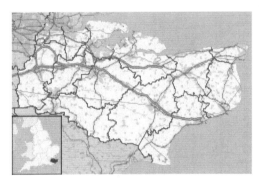

Dymchurch has had a sea wall since Roman times, with the original development being constructed to protect the harbour at Port Lympne., and then continuing throughout the centuries to help protect the Marsh itself.

knolls – a small round hill.

the wire – the telephone wire carrying messages from Romney to Hythe.

The Straits – the Straits of Dover. The English Channel.

the offing – the area between the shore and the horizon.

brands – lit pieces of wood used as torches.

Who? The poet describes the beauty of Romney Marsh, but does not let his personality intrude at all.

When? The late nineteenth century.

Where? Romney Marsh.

What? In this largely descriptive poem, Davidson concentrates on the sights and sounds of the marsh.

Commentary

The title of the poem '**In** Romney Marsh' suggests Davidson's complete immersion in the marsh. This is not just a poem about Romney Marsh: the word 'in' suggests that from within the marsh Davidson is able fully to appreciate the natural world of the marsh: he is absorbed in it and part of it. Davidson writes in four line stanzas - quatrains – in which the first and the third lines rhyme and the second and the fourth. This highly traditional and controlled form suggests that Davidson is fully in control of his material; it also strongly suggests the perfect beauty of the scene. – nothing spoils the beauty of the scene, just as nothing spoils the perfection and controlled order of the poem.

Much of the poem details what Davidson can see and hear and he is alive to the natural phenomena on the marsh as well as the human. In the first stanza Davidson says he 'went down to Dymchurch Wall' and he writes that he

…heard the South sing o'er the land

I saw the yellow sunlight fall

On knolls where Norman churches stand.

The south wind is personified as it sings over the flat land and the yellow sunlight suggests warmth and brightness. The Norman churches suggest the history and antiquity of the area. Already in the first stanza Davidson's senses are heightened and much of the poem consists of what he hears and what he sees – his senses are highly attuned to his surroundings.

In the second stanza Davidson can hear the telephone wire carrying messages from Romney to Hythe – and he can hear it 'ringing shrilly, taut and lithe/Within the wind a core of sound'. Perhaps the wire is reverberating in the wind. Ringing shrilly is a sharp and penetrating sound. The 'airy journey' perfectly describes the journey that the words on the telephone make.

The third stanza switches to the sense of sight and Davidson notices 'A veil of purple vapour' out at sea, while the upper air

... like sapphire glowed.

And roses filled Heaven's gates.

This is an especially beautiful stanza, helped by the poetic techniques that Davidson uses: the metaphor of the 'veil of purple vapour' is augmented by the simile – 'The upper air like sapphire glowed' – and the whole stanza is rounded off by the unusual and original image of the roses filling Heaven's gates. Davidson is overwhelmed by the natural beauty of the sky above the Marsh.

In the fourth stanza Davidson turns to the shoreline and begins by personifying the masts who 'wagged their tops' in the wind, which makes them sound playful. The rest of the stanza concentrates on the sound and visual qualities of the waves hitting the shore. 'Pealed', 'surge' and 'roar' are all onomatopoeic, while 'saffron' and 'diamond' suggest how beautiful and precious the beach and the waves are, while 'beads' is a metaphor related to jewellery which describes the drops of water being flung up the shore.

The fifth stanza marks a break and a reversal of the first line of the poem. Now Davidson writes

As I came up from Dymchurch Wall

and evening is approaching. In a metaphor Davidson describes the fiery and beautiful sunset:

The crimson brands of sunset fall,

Flicker and fade from out the West.

The personified 'crimson brands' suggest that the sky is streaked with red, while the alliteration that follows on the letter 'f' emphasizes the movement of the colours in the sky.

The first line of the sixth stanza begins with a strong caesura after 'Night sank' which emphasizes its speed. Davidson follows this with a simile – 'like flakes of silver fire' which once again evokes precious metals and accentuates the beauty of the stars which 'in one great shower came down' – and the enjambment between lines one and two of the stanza stresses the speed at which the stars descended. Davidson is still attuned to the noises around him. The wind is shrill and the wire is shrill and the wire 'Rang out'. 'Shrill' and 'rang' are both onomatopoeic.

The final stanza returns to the shore line to describe vividly the waves crashing on the beach:

The darkly shining salt sea drops

Streamed as the waves clashed on the shore

In these two lines the sibilance on the letter 's' and the onomatopoeic 'clashed' give an accurate sense of the sound of the sea. And in the final two lines the beach is compared in a metaphor to an organ with 'pealing' and 'roar' both being onomatopoeic.

The tone of this intensely vivid poem is admiring and full of a love and fascination with this place.

In 'In Romney Marsh' John Davidson

- makes clear his love and closeness to the landscape;
- makes extensive use of metaphor, simile and onomatopoeia to bring the landscape alive;

- has all his senses attuned to the sights and sounds of Romney Marsh;
- gives a vivid and evocative sense of Romney Marsh.

'Absence' – Elizabeth Jennings

Author and Context

Jennings was born in Boston, Lincolnshire. When she was six, her family moved to Oxford, where she remained for the rest of her life.[2] There she later attended St Anne's College. After graduation, she became a writer. Jennings' early poetry was published in journals such as *Oxford Poetry*, *New English Weekly*, *The Spectator*, *Outposts* and *Poetry Review*, but her first book was not published until she was 27. The lyrical poets whom she usually cited as having greatly influenced her work were Hopkins, Auden, Graves and Muir. Her second book, *A Way of Looking*, won the Somerset Maugham award and marked a turning point, as the prize money allowed her to spend nearly three months in Rome, which was a revelation. It brought a new dimension to her religious belief and inspired her imagination.

Regarded as traditionalist rather than an innovator, Jennings is known for her lyric poetry and mastery of form. Her work displays a simplicity of metre and rhyme shared with Philip Larkin, Kingsley Amis and Thom Gunn, all members of the group of English poets known as The Movement. She always made it clear that, whilst her life, which included a spell of severe mental illness, contributed to the themes contained within her work, she did not write explicitly autobiographical poetry. Her deeply held Roman Catholicism coloured much of her work.

She died in a care home in Bampton, Oxfordshire and is buried in Wolvercote Cemetery, Oxford.

Who? The poet writes as herself and addresses her former lover or companion.

When? In summer perhaps – there are lots of birds singing.

Where? The place is not specified except as the place where she and a former lover last met and ended their relationship.

What? The poet reflects on the beauty and serenity of her surroundings contrasted with the emotional turmoil she feels inside.

Commentary

This is a sad and melancholy poem. It is based on a place – which is as attractive and as beautiful as it ever was – but the speaker of the poem is there alone – without her companion or lover – and so her perceptions and feelings have changed completely.

In the first stanza the speaker visits *the place where we last met* alone, we assume the relationship has ended. Ironically nothing has changed which must sharpen the memory of their last visit there:

Nothing was changed, the gardens were well-tended,

The fountains sprayed their usual steady jet;

The poet writes that *there was no sign that anything had ended/ And nothing to instruct me to forget*. It's almost as if had the place fallen to rack and ruin that would have been an appropriate metaphor for the breakdown in their relationship. It's also galling in the breakup of a relationship that a special place with particular connotations continues to thrive. As it is the place the poet revisits is as nice as it ever was. The relationship and its ending has had a profound effect on the poet and she wants something to instruct her to forget.

In the second stanza the *thoughtless birds* are *singing an ecstasy I could not share.* They are thoughtless because they do not, cannot, take into account her feelings of misery. In the second half of the second stanza Jennings admits that faced with the beauty of the birdsong she should feel no *pain* or *discord*.

However, in the third stanza Jennings allows the depths of her sorrow to become apparent. She starts by saying:

It was because the place was just the same

That made your absence seem a savage force.

The place has not changed but their relationship has. She then imagines that underneath the essential gentleness of the scene – the fountains, the trees, the birds, the well-tended gardens – there comes an *earthquake tremor* when she thinks of her former lover's name.

The overall tone of this poem is relatively calm until we reach the cataclysmic events of the last stanza. This is, in part, because Jennings uses a conventional rhyme scheme which gives the poem order and shape. However, it is important to note that as the poem becomes more emotional in stanzas two and three, Jennings uses more enjambment to increase the emotional momentum of her words. However, nothing prepares us for the *earthquake tremor* of the last verse. Because the place is unchanged it is almost as if Jennings wants to destroy it, so that she can at the same time destroy the once-happy memories she had of the place.

In this poem Elizabeth Jennings:

- revisits a place she had once visited with a former lover – this time she is alone;
- she seems cheated to find that the place has not changed, although time has changed her relationship;
- restrains her emotions (through a tight and regular rhyme scheme) until the last verse where she admits the intense sadness she feels.

Glossary

The Oxford Concise Dictionary of Literary Terms has been invaluable in writing this section of the book. I would again remind the reader that knowledge of these terms is only the start – do NOT define a word you find here in the examination. You can take it for granted that the examiner knows the term: it is up to you to try to use it confidently and with precision and to explain why the poet uses it or what effect it has on the reader.

ALLITERATION
: the repetition of the same sounds – usually initial consonants or stressed syllables – in any sequence of closely adjacent words.

ALLUSION
: an indirect or passing reference to some event, person, place or artistic work which is not explained by the writer, but which relies on the reader's familiarity with it.

AMBIGUITY
: openness to different interpretations.

ANAPAEST
: a metrical foot made up of two unstressed syllables followed by a stressed syllable.

ANAPHORA
: the repetition of a word or a phrase at the start of consecutive lines of poetry, or clauses, or sentences.

ASSONANCE
: the repetition of similar vowel sounds in neighbouring words.

BALLAD
: a folk song or orally transmitted poem telling in a simple and direct way a story with a tragic ending. Ballads are normally composed in quatrains with the second and fourth lines rhyming. Such quatrains are known as the ballad stanza because of its frequent use in what we call

ballads.

BLANK VERSE   unrhymed lines of ten syllable length. This is a widely used form by Shakespeare in his plays, by Milton and by Wordsworth.

CAESURA   any pause in a line of verse caused by punctuation. This can draw attention to what precedes or follows the caesura and also, by breaking up the rhythm of the line, can slow the poem down and make it more like ordinary speech.

CANON   a body of writings recognized by authority. The canon of a national literature is a body of writings especially approved by critics or anthologists and deemed suitable for academic study. Towards the end of the 20th century there was a general feeling that the canon of English Literature was dominated by dead white men and since then there has been a deliberate and fruitful attempt made to give more prominence to writing by women and by writers from non-white backgrounds. Even your Anthology is a contribution to the canon, because someone sat down and decided that the poems included in it were worthy of study by students taking GCSE.

CARPE DIEM   a Latin phrase from the Roman poet Horace which means 'seize the day' – 'make the best of the present moment'. It is a very common theme of European lyric poetry, in which the speaker of a poem argues that since time is short and death is inevitable, pleasure should be enjoyed while there is still time.

COLLOCATION	the act of putting two words together. What this means in practice is that certain words have very common collocations – in other words they are usually found in written or spoken English in collocation with other words. For example, the word *Christmas* is often collocated with words such as *cards*, *presents*, *carols*, *holidays*, but you won't often find it collocated with *sadness*. This can be an important term because poets, who are seeking to use words in original ways, will often put two words together which are not often collocated.
COLLOQUIALISM	the use of informal expressions or vocabulary appropriate to everyday speech rather than the formality of writing. When used in poetry it can make the poem seem more down-to-earth and real, more honest and intimate.
CONCEIT	an unusually far-fetched metaphor presenting a surprising and witty parallel between two apparently dissimilar things or feelings.
CONSONANCE	the repetition of identical or similar consonants in neighbouring words whose vowel sounds are different.
CONTEXT	the biographical, social, cultural and historical circumstances in which a text is produced and read and understood – you might to like tothink of it as its background. However, it is important sometimes to consider the reader's own context – especially when we look back at poems from the Literary Heritage. To interpret a poem with full regard to its background is to contextualize it.

COUPLET

a pair of rhyming verse lines, usually of the same length.

CROSSED RHYME

the rhyming of one word in the middle of a long line of poetry with a word in a similar position in the next line.

DACTYL

a metrical foot having two unstressed syllables followed by a stressed syllable.

DIALECT

a distinctive variety of language, spoken by members of an identifiable regional group, nation or social class. Dialects differ from one another in pronunciation, vocabulary and grammar. Traditionally they have been looked down on and viewed as variations from an educated 'standard' form of the language, but linguists point out that standard forms themselves are merely dialects which have come to dominate for social and political reasons. In English this notion of dialect is especially important because English is spoken all over the world and there are variations between the English spoken in, say, Yorkshire, Delhi and Australia. Dialects now are increasingly celebrated as a distinct way of speaking and writing which are integral to our identity.

DICTION

the choice of words used in any literary work.

DISSONANCE

harshness of sound.

DRAMATIC MONOLOGUE

a kind of poem in which a single fictional or historical character (not the poet) speaks to a silent audience and unwittingly reveals the truth about their character.

ELEGY a lyric poem lamenting the death of a friend or public figure or reflecting seriously on a serious subject. The elegiac has come to refer to the mournful mood of such poems.

ELLIPSIS the omission from a sentence of a word or words which would be required for complete clarity. It is used all the time in everyday speech, but is often used in poetry to promote compression and/or ambiguity. The adjective is elliptical.

END-RHYME rhyme occurring at the end of a line of poetry. The most common form of rhyme.

END-STOPPED a line of poetry brought to a pause by the use of punctuation. The opposite of enjambment.

ENJAMBMENT caused by the lack of punctuation at the end of a line of poetry, this causes the sense (and the voice when the poem is read aloud) to 'run over' into the next line. In general, this can impart to poems the feel of ordinary speech, but there are examples in the Anthology of more precise reasons for the poet to use enjambment.

EPIPHANY a sudden moment of insight or revelation, usually at the end of a poem.

EPIZEUXIS the technique by which a word is repeated for emphasis with no other words intervening

EUPHONY a pleasing smoothness of sound

FALLING RHTHYM   a rhythmical effect in which the end of the lines of a poem consist of trochees or dactyls. The effect is often of uncertainty or poignancy, but it can also be used for comic effect.

FEMININE

ENDING   any line of poetry which ends on an unstressed syllable and which ensures the line ends on a falling rhythm.

FIGURATIVE   Not literal. Obviously 'figurative' language covers metaphor and simile and personification

FIGURE OF SPEECH   any expression which departs from the ordinary literal sense or normal order of words. Figurative language (the opposite of literal language) includes metaphor, simile and personification. Some figures of speech – such as alliteration and assonance achieve their effects through the repetition of sounds.

FOREGROUNDING   giving unusual prominence to one part of a text. Poetry differs from everyday speech and prose by its use of regular rhythm, metaphors, alliteration and other devices by which its language draws attention to itself.

FREE VERSE   a kind of poetry that does not conform to any regular pattern of line length or rhyme. The length of its lines are irregular as is its use of rhyme – if any.

HALF-RHYME   an imperfect rhyme – also known as para-rhyme, near rhyme and slant rhyme – in which the final consonants match but the vowel sounds do not match. Pioneered in the 19th century by the Emily Dickinson and Gerard Manley Hopkins, and made even more popular by Wilfred Owen and T S Eliot in the early 20th century,

HOMONYM a word that is identical to another word either in sound or in spelling

HOMOPHONE a word that is pronounced in the same way as another word but which differs in meaning and/or spelling.

HYPERBOLE exaggeration for the sake of emphasis.

IAMB a metrical foot of verse having one unstressed syllable followed by one stressed. Lines made up predominately of iambs are referred to as iambics or iambic verse. The 10 syllable iambic pentameter (rhymed or unrhymed) is the most common line in English poetry. The 8 syllable iambic tetrameter is also very popular. The 12 syllable iambic hexameter is less common in English and is also known as the alexandrine. Even if the rhythm of a poem is predominately iambic, it does not preclude metrical variation – often with a trochaic foot at the start of a line to give maximum impact.

IDIOM an everyday phrase that cannot be translated literally because its meaning does not correspond to the specific words in the phrase. There are thousands in English like – *you get up my nose, when pigs fly, she was all ears.*

IMAGERY a rather vague critical term covering literal and

metaphorical language which evoke sense impressions with reference to concrete objects – the things the writer describes.

INTERNAL RHYME   a poetic device in which two or more words in the same line rhyme.

INTERTEXTUALITY   the relationship that a text may have with another preceding and usually well-known text.

INVERSION   the reversal of the normally expected order or words. 'Normally expected' means how we might say the words in the order of normal speech; to invert the normal word order usually draws attention or foregrounds the words.

JUXTAPOSITION   two things that are placed alongside each other.

LAMENT   any poem expressing profound grief usually in the face of death.

LATINATE   Latinate diction in English means the use of words derived from Latin rather than those derived from Old English.

LITOTES   understatement – the opposite of hyperbole.

LYRIC   any fairly short poem expressing the personal mood of the speaker.

MASCULINE ENDING   Any line of poetry which ends on a stressed syllable.

METAPHOR   the most important figure of speech in which in which one thing is referred to by a word normally associated with another thing, so as to suggest some common quality shared by both things. In metaphor, this similarity is directly stated, unlike in a simile where the resemblance is indirect and introduced by the words like or as. Much of our everyday language is made up of metaphor too – to say someone is as greedy as a pig is a simile; to say he is a pig is a metaphor.

MNEMONIC a form of words or letters that helps people remember things. It is common in everyday sayings and uses some of the features of language that we associate with poetry. For example, the weather saying Red sky at night, shepherd's delight uses rhyme.

MONOLOGUE` an extended speech uttered by one speaker.

NARRATOR the one who tells or is assumed to be the voice of the poem.

OCTAVE or OCTET a group of eight lines forming the first part of a sonnet.

ONOMATOPOEIA the use of words that seem to imitate the sounds they refer to (*bang, whizz, crackle, fizz*) or any combination or words in which the sound echoes or seems to echo the sense. The adjective is onomatopoeic, so you can say that *blast* is an onomatopoeic word.

ORAL TRADITION the passing on from one generation to another of songs, chants, poems, proverbs by word of mouth and memory.

OXYMORON a figure of speech that combines two seemingly contradictory terms as in the everyday terms bitter-sweet and living-death.

PARALLELISM the arrangement of similarly constructed clause, sentences or lines of poetry.

PARADOX a statement which is self-contradictory.

PATHETIC FALLACY this is the convention that natural phenomena (usually the weather) are a reflection of the poet's or the narrator's mood. It may well involve the personification of things in nature, but does not have to. At its simplest, a writer might choose to associate very bad weather with a mood of depression and sadness.

PERSONA the assumed identity or fictional narrator assumed by a writer.

PERSONIFICATION a figure of speech in which animals, abstract ideas or lifeless things are referred to as if they were human. Sometimes known as personal metaphor.

PETRARCHAN characteristic of the Italian poet Petrarch (1304 – 1374). Mainly applied to the Petrarchan sonnet which is different in its form from the Shakespearean sonnet.

PHONETIC SPELLING a technique writers use which involves misspelling a word in order to imitate the accent in which the word is said.

PLOSIVE explosive. Used to describe sounds that we form by putting our lips together such as *b* and *p*.

POSTCOLONIAL LITERATURE a term devised to describe what used to be called Commonwealth Literature (and before that Empire Writing!). The term covers a very wide range of writing from countries that were once colonies of European countries. It has come to include some writing by writers of non-white racial backgrounds whose roots or family originated in former colonies – no matter where they live now.

PUN an expression that derives humour either through using a word that has two distinct meanings or two similar sounding words (homophones).

QUATRAIN a verse stanza of four lines – usually rhymed.

REFRAIN a line, or a group of lines, repeated at intervals throughout a poem – usually at regular intervals and at the end of a stanza.

RHYME the identity of sound between syllables or paired groups of syllables usually at the end of a line of poetry.

RHYME SCHEME the pattern in which the rhymed line endings are arranged in any poem or stanza. This is normally written as a sequence of letters where each line ending in the same rhyme is given the same alphabetical letter. So a Shakespearean sonnet's rhyme scheme is ababcdcdefefgg, but the rhyme scheme of a Petrarchan sonnet is abbaabbacdecde. In other poems the rhyme scheme might be arranged to suit the poet's convenience or intentions. For example, in Blake's 'London' the first stanza rhymes abab, the second cdcd and so on.

RHYTHM   a pattern of sounds which is repeated with the stress falling on the same syllables (more or less) in each line. However, variations to the pattern, especially towards the end of the poem, often stand out and are foregrounded because they break the pattern the poet has built up through the course of the poem.

ROMANTICISM   the name given to the artistic movement that emerged in England and Germany in the 1790s and in the rest of Europe in the 1820s and beyond. It was a movement that saw great changes in literature, painting, sculpture, architecture and music and found its catalyst in the new philosophical ideas of Jean Jacques Rousseau and Thomas Paine, and in response to the French and industrial revolutions. Its chief emphasis was on freedom of individual self-expression, sincerity, spontaneity and originality, but it also looked to the distant past of the Middle Ages for some of its inspiration.

SATIRE   any type of writing which exposes and mocks the foolishness or evil of individuals, institutions or societies. A poem can be satiric (adjective) or you can say a poet satirizes something or somebody.

SESTET   a group of six lines forming the second half of a sonnet, following the octet.

SIBILANCE   the noticeable recurrence of *s* sounds.

SIMILE	an explicit comparison between two different things, actions or feelings, usually introduced by *like* or *as*.
SONNET	a lyric poem of 14 lines of equal length. The form originated in Italy and was made famous as a vehicle for love poetry by Petrarch and came to be adopted throughout Europe. The standard subject matter of early sonnets was romantic love, but in the 17th century John Donne used it to write religious poetry and John Milton wrote political sonnets, so it came to be used for any subject matter. The sonnet form enjoyed a revival in the Romantic period (Wordsworth, Keats and Shelley all wrote them) and continues to be widely used today. Some poets have written connected series of sonnets and these are known as sonnet cycles. Petrarchan sonnets differ slightly in their rhyme scheme from Shakespearean sonnets (see the entry above on rhyme scheme). A Petrarchan sonnet consists of two quatrains (the octet) followed by two tercets (the sestet). A Shakespearean sonnet consists of two quatrains (the octet) followed by another quatrain and a final couplet (the sestet).
SPONDEE	a metrical unit consisting of two stressed syllables.
STANZA	a group of verse lines forming a section of a poem and sharing the same structure in terms of the length of the lines, the rhyme scheme and the rhythm.
STYLE	any specific way of using language, which is characteristic of an author, a period, a type of poetry or a group of writers.

SYLLOGISM	a form of logical argument that draws a conclusion from two propositions.
SYMBOL	anything that represents something else. A national flag symbolizes the country that uses it; symbols are heavily used in road signs. In poetry symbols can represent almost anything. Blake's 'The Sick Rose' is a good example of a poem which uses a symbol.
SYNECDOCHE	a figure of speech in which a thing or person is referred to indirectly, either by naming some part of it (*hands* for manual labourers) or by naming some big thing of which it is a part (the law for police officers). As you can see from these examples, it is a common practice in speech.
TONE	a critical term meaning the mood or atmosphere of a piece of writing. It may also include the sense of the writer's attitude to the reader of the subject matter.
TROCHEE	a metrical foot having a stressed syllable followed by an unstressed syllable.
TURN	the English term for a sudden change in mood or line of argument, especially in line 9 of a sonnet.
VERSE	another word for poetry as opposed to prose. The use of the word 'verse' sometimes implies writing that rhymes and has a rhythm, but perhaps lacks the merit of real poetry.
VERSE PARAGRAPH	a group of lines of poetry forming a section of a poem, the length of the unit being determined by the sense rather than a particular stanza pattern.

VOLTA   the Italian term for the 'turn' in the argument or mood of a sonnet which normally occurs in the ninth line at the start of the sestet, but sometimes in Shakespearean sonnets is delayed until the final couplet.

WIT   a general term which covers the idea of intelligence, but refers in poetry more specifically to verbal ingenuity and cleverness.